SIKHISM
A new approach

Pamela Draycott

Hodder & Stoughton
A MEMBER OF THE HODDER HEADLINE GROUP

Acknowledgements

The Publishers would like to thank the following for permission to reproduce copyright illustrations: p24 top left, p68, The British Sikh Education Council; p24 right and bottom, p25 left, Pamela Draycott; p9, p58, p85, David Rose; p50, p64 bottom, Mel Thompson. All the other photographs were supplied by Philip Emmett.

The artwork in this book is by
Dharmachari Aloka

Author's Acknowledgements

I would like to say a special word of thanks to Sikh friends, acquaintances and colleagues for their willingness to share insights into their faith, without which this book not only would not but could not have been written. Also to my husband, John, and daughter, Emily, for their love, patience and encouragement in this endeavour.

To Joan Charlesworth, an inspiring RE teacher

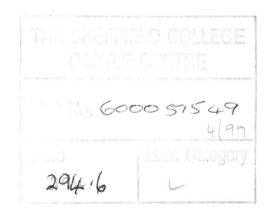

British Library Cataloguing in Publication Data

Draycott, Pamela
Sikhism: a new approach
1. Sikhism
I. Title
249.6

ISBN 0 340 60555 3

First published 1996
Impression number   10 9 8 7 6 5 4 3 2 1
Year   1999 1998 1997 1996

Printed for Hodder & Stoughton Educational, a division of Hodder Headline Plc, 338 Euston Road, London NW1 3BH by Bath Press Colourbooks, Glasgow.

Contents

Teacher's Introduction

Sikhism: A new approach is an exploration of the Sikh way of life, which focuses on both belief and practice. It offers a basic outline and insights into this principal religious tradition. As a belief system the Sikh faith offers adherents a complete way of life, affecting the things people do, the way people think, their beliefs, values and attitudes. It is important that students are given opportunities to develop their understanding of this, so this publication seeks to address not only what Sikhs do but why they do it.

Although chapters in this publication can be used in numerical sequence, the teacher will need to decide if that is the most suitable order for particular groups of students to explore the Sikh faith. With this in mind, the chapters are to some extent self-contained, and may be used independently of each other.

English spellings of Sikh terms are based on those provided by the School Curriculum and Assessment Authority in their Glossary of Terms (ISBN 1 85838 041 3), 1994.

These words from the Guru Granth Sahib, translated from the Punjabi, encapsulate something of the teaching of the Gurus. They are offered to provide food for thought.

Make chastity your furnace, patience your smithy,
The Master's word your anvil, and true knowledge your hammer.
Make awe of God your bellows, and with it kindle the fire of austerity.
And in the crucible of love, melt the nectar Divine.
Only in such a mint, can man be cast into the Word.

A note about this series

The 'new approach' series of textbooks seeks to offer the core of factual information required for GCSE examinations, but to do so in the context of the broader aims of religious education at Key Stage 4 and above. It therefore attempts to present a balance between the factual and the experiential approaches to religion.

This balance reflects the conviction that one can only understand a religion once one has allowed its teachings, at least to some extent, to inform and challenge one's own view of life. Equally, a personal quest for insight and meaning cannot but benefit from an examination of the teachings of the world's great religions.

Student's Introduction

The Sikh faith is one of the youngest of the world's religions. It does not claim a monopoly on truth, seeing things of worth in other faiths and seeking co-existence with them.

It emphasises equality, for example, between men and women and between people of different social groupings.

To be a Sikh is to follow the teachings of the Gurus by putting them into practice in everyday life, particularly in the selfless service of others.

This book will outline for you the beliefs and practices which form the foundation for the Sikh way of life.

1

Sikhism - A Living Faith

- Origins
- Sikhs in Britain Today
- Sikh Movements

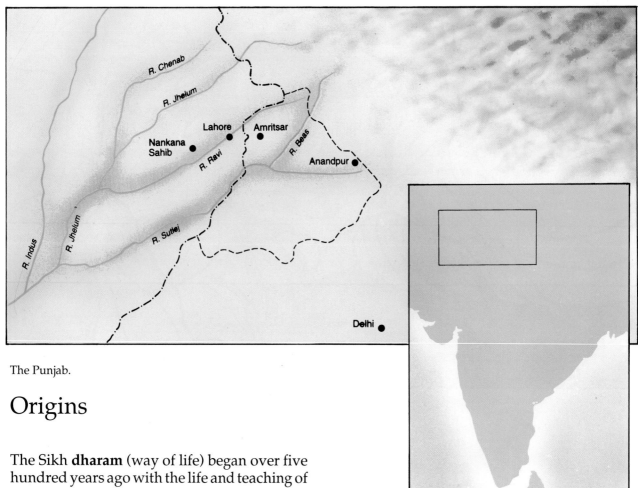

The Punjab.

Origins

The Sikh **dharam** (way of life) began over five hundred years ago with the life and teaching of Guru Nanak and his successors (see chapter 2). It is therefore one of the youngest of the world's religions. Numerically it is also relatively small. There are approximately 19,000,000 Sikhs, the majority of whom (around 80 per cent) live, where it began, in the northern Indian state of Punjab.

The Punjab is a fertile region served by five rivers - the Jhelum, Chenab, Ravi, Beas and Sutlej - which all flow into the River Indus. The word 'Punjab' means 'Five streams'.

Some key facts:

- Sikh population world-wide – 19,000,000 (approximately)

- Major centre of Sikh population – Northern Indian state of Punjab, where about 80 per cent of total Sikh population live

- Other places with significant Sikh populations – India, Britain, USA, East Africa Malaysia, Singapore

- First **Guru** and 'founder' of the Sikh faith – Guru Nanak (1469-1539 CE)

Two important terms:
- *'Sikh'* – From Punjabi word 'sishya' which means 'learner' or 'disciple'
- *'Dharam'* – Way of life

- Sikhs believe that their faith is a way of life, a religion, revealed through the life and teaching of Guru Nanak, his nine human successors and the Guru Granth Sahib.

- Sikhs believe that Guru Nanak was born in an enlightened state and that when he was around 30 years old he received his call from God to preach a message of love, peace and equality centred on the worship of God. He travelled extensively to spread his message undertaking four long journeys (called Udasi) before settling in Kartarpur.

- He was succeeded by nine other Gurus whom Sikhs believe to have all conveyed the same message. The tenth Guru, Guru Gobind Singh said that the scriptures, the Guru Granth Sahib, was to succeed him as the living word of God.

- Sikhs believe in one God, **Akal Purakh**, the eternal God, who has revealed himself continuously since before the coming of the ten Gurus and continues to do so today through the Guru Granth Sahib.

- Sikhs believe that this one God is known by many names but the two traditionally used by Sikhs in worship are Satnam and Raheguru. Belief in this one God, who created countless universes, should lead adherents to worship, by meditating on the divine name, and to service, of God and of humanity.

- Since God is the creator of all and humanity is the supreme form of created life, human beings should treat all equally and with respect.

Belief in the oneness of God and in the oneness of humanity, leads to a belief in the equality of all, a tolerance towards other religions and a willingness to act in the service of humanity.

Sikhs in Britain Today

Although some Sikhs lived in Britain earlier, (indeed the first gurdwara was opened in Putney, in south east London in 1911) the majority settled in the 1950s and 1960s. Outside of India, Britain has the largest Sikh community but there are also sizeable communities in Canada, the United States of America and East Africa.

It is estimated that today there are around 400,000 Sikhs living in Britain, many of them in larger towns and cities such as Birmingham, Bradford, Cardiff, Glasgow, Leicester and London (particularly Southall). There are over 180 gurdwaras around the country.

The majority of Sikhs living in Britain have direct links with the Punjab through relations and friends who live there. Many of them, or their parents or grandparents, came to Britain directly from the Punjab. Some, however, came in the early 1970s after being expelled from Uganda by its then leader, Idi Amin.

Sikhs have migrated to many Commonwealth and English-speaking countries because of their historic links with the British Empire. In the late nineteenth century, Sikhs were among those who went to Africa with the British to help in the development of their colonies. Today there are few Sikhs left in Uganda but Kenya still has a sizeable Sikh population.

Employment

Many male Sikhs have served in the British Army both in India and abroad. On coming to Britain, Sikhs began work in many of the areas in which there was, at that time, a shortage of workers - transport, textiles, etc. Some became involved in the retail trade and others in the food industry - shops, market stalls and restaurants. Many are doctors, lawyers or teachers. Indeed today members of the Sikh faith can be found in many walks of life.

Education

Education is an important aspect of Sikh life. The Guru Nanak Sikh College, in Hayes, Middlesex was opened at the beginning of 1993 as a mixed independent college with about four hundred children from nursery to GCSE level. There are also plans to add a sixth form. It is the first Sikh College in Europe and was founded by Sant Bab Amar Singh, the chairman and spiritual head of the Nanak Sar Thath Ishar Darbar organisation. The majority of its pupils

Education is an important feature of the life of a gurdwara. Young people are taught Punjabi.

are Sikh but there are also pupils who belong to other faith traditions studying at the school. Sikh worship is a regular part of the life of the college and Punjabi is taught as part of the curriculum.

In Britain the vast majority of children and young people are educated in schools which do not have a Sikh foundation and consequently many do not have the opportunity to learn Punjabi at school. Many visit the gurdwara on a regular basis to take part in Punjabi classes. This enables them to better understand worship (since worship is based on readings and singing from the Holy Granth). Some Sikh adults are concerned that if children do not learn Punjabi they will be unable to take a full part in family life, since some family members will have Punjabi as their first language. Some gurdwaras also provide classes where children and young people have the opportunity to learn to play one or more of the traditional musical instruments used in worship.

Fact Box

A **gurdwara** is a Sikh place of worship. In Great Britain gurdwaras often act as community centres and places where children and young people are taught Punjabi.

Worship

There is no set day of the week which is regarded as holy by Sikhs, but in this country the major services of the week are likely to be on a Sunday since that is the day when most people are not at work. Many gurdwaras are open daily and some Sikhs would visit in the morning before going to work or in the evening after work.

Equality

The Sikh faith teaches that there are no distinctions between people, in terms of sex, age or social grouping. The caste system was rejected by Guru Nanak and since then equality, between the sexes and between people of different social, economic or employment groupings, has been an important element of the Sikh way of life.

Religion consists not in mere talk. He who looks on all alike and considers all to be equal is acclaimed as truly religious.

Adi Granth 730

We are God's own people, neither high nor low nor in between.

Adi Granth 504

Sikh Groups

There are no denominations as such within the Sikh faith but there are some Sikhs who follow more closely the example of a particular Sikh leader. For example, in the USA, a Sikh leader, Har Bhajan Singh Yogi taught meditation. Some of those who came to learn from him became Sikh. They live together in ashrams, wear white clothing and both sexes wear the turban.

In some gurdwaras a particular group may predominate. There are three basic groups which have their origins in different occupational backgrounds - bhattras, jats and ramgarhias. Traditionally bhattras were traders, jats were farmers and ramgarhias were craft workers but today members of each group tend to be employed in a wide range of occupations. However, there is still something of a tendancy for groups not to intermarry.

Sikh Movements

There have been three important Sikh movements which have contributed to the Sikh way of life as it is today. These movements are the Nirankaris, the Namdharis and the Singh Sabha Movement.

The Nirankaris

Dayal Das was a deeply spiritual man, devoted to God. He believed that worship was central to life and that the Guru Granth Sahib was central to worship. He was appalled to find that Sikhs were being married according to Hindu practices rather than by Sikh practices in the presence of the Guru Granth Sahib. He began a campaigning and reforming movement which encouraged all Sikhs to have naming and marriage ceremonies based around the Guru Granth Sahib, as he believed the Gurus had taught.

They became known as the Nirankaris because Dayal Das described Guru Nanak as 'Nanak nirankar' - the formless one. 'Nirankar' is a name which Guru Nanak sometimes used to refer to God.

Dayal Das died in the year 1855 CE. Much of what he and his followers wanted was achieved with the passing of the Anand Marriage Act in 1909, which gave Sikhs the legal right to conduct their own wedding ceremonies and the Gurdwara Act of 1925 which gave them control of the gurdwaras.

The Namdharis

Baba Ram Singh was the leader of a reforming movement which called Sikhs back to the traditional principles laid down for them by their Gurus.

He found, for example, that some Sikhs had started to drink alcohol and smoke tobacco as well as to eat meat killed in the halal way - all forbidden by the Gurus. He also found that some were demanding large dowries when getting married which again went against what the Gurus had laid down.

He sought to encourage people to live by the simple principles of the faith.

Around seventy of his followers were accused of having taken part in agitation which had resulted in riots. They were executed by the British rulers.

Baba Ram Singh was exiled to Burma in 1872 and he died in 1885CE.

The Singh Sabha Movement

The Singh Sabha Movement did not begin as a means of reforming the Sikh faith or encouraging Sikhs to be more faithful to their way of life, but as a response to the missionary activities of other faiths.

During the nineteenth century Christian missions were set up in the Punjab and surrounding districts, with the expressed intention of converting people to the Christian faith. In the 1870s a Hindu movement with the aim of countering Christian missionary activitiy and bringing about a Hindu revival was launched. It had the effect of converting some Muslims and Sikhs to the Hindu faith.

The Singh Sabha Movement sprang up in response to these activities. Its main interest was in Sikh educational, social and religious work. It brought about the removal of Hindu statues which had been placed in some gurdwaras and ensured that gurdwaras stayed open to all Sikhs regardless of caste. Schools to teach the faith were established. The Khalsa College in Amritsar was opened in 1892.

As a result of this movement more Sikhs took part in the Amrit Sanskar (the Sikh rite of initiation into the Khalsa) and took to wearing the Panj Kakke (the Five Ks) as an expression of their faith.

Activities

Key Elements

1 Approximately how many Sikhs are there world-wide?

2 Approximately how many Sikhs live in Great Britain?

3 In which region did the Sikh faith originate?

4 What does the word 'Sikh' mean?

5 What are bhattras, jats and ramgarhias?

6 On which day of the week are the major weekly worship services held? Is this the same in other countries?

7 What is a gurdwara?

Think About It

8 The Sikh faith emphasises the equality of all people, based on belief in one God. How do you think that might be worked out in practice in everyday life?

9 Why do you think it is important to many Sikhs in this country for their children to learn Punjabi?

Assignments

1 Using pages 6 and 7 as a starting point find out more about and make notes on:
a) The world-wide Sikh community - numbers, places, influence, etc.
b) The Punjab - where it is, its climate, economy and government, its importance within the Sikh community.

2 Using pages 10 and 11 as a starting point find out more about and make notes on:
a) The Nirankaris and Dayal Das.
b) The Namdharis and Baba Ram Singh.
c) The Singh Sabha Movement.

3 If possible, conduct an interview with a Sikh to find out something about how their faith affects the way in which they live.

2

The Ten Gurus

- Introduction
- The Lives and Teachings of the Gurus
- The Importance of the Gurus within Sikhism Today

Introduction

The Sikh faith was revealed through ten Gurus (religious teachers) who lived in northern India between the mid fifteenth and very early seventeenth centuries CE. They claimed that their teaching came directly from God and that it was God who gave them the authority to teach and proclaim it.

The basis of their message was that there is only one God, the creator, carer and sustainer of all. People of all castes, men and women, rich and poor are equally important to God and may receive spiritual liberation (moksha) in this present life as they respond in love and faithful obedience to God.

Fact Box

Sikhs believe that the Gurus' teachings provide a framework to help them live their lives in a way which is pleasing to God.

Each of the Gurus is regarded as equally important, since all are messengers of God. They are revered (highly respected) by Sikhs but not worshipped by them. However, they are regarded as belonging to a special class of person who have no need to be reborn because of past deeds (see page 43 for an explanation of this belief) but who come back to earth because God wants them to be his messengers. Sikhs honour their own Gurus but are also prepared to recognise others (for example the Buddha or Jesus) as ones who were sent into the world to reveal God's message.

The line of living Gurus ended with Guru Gobind Singh who said that there were to be no more earthly successors to him but that the holy book (the Adi Granth/Guru Granth Sahib) should become the Guru.

The Ten Gurus

1 Guru Nanak (1469-1539)

2 Guru Angad (1539-52)

3 Guru Amar Das (1552-74)

4 Guru Ram Das (1574-81)

5 Guru Arjan (1581-1606)

6 Guru Hargobind (1606-44)

7 Guru Har Rai (1644-61)

8 Guru Har Krishan (1661-4)

9 Guru Tegh Bahadur (1664-75)

10 Guru Gobind Singh (1675-1708)

Each of the ten Gurus contributed something to the formation of the Sikh faith and community. They are remembered for the things they taught and the way in which they lived their lives. They are important to Sikhs as examples to follow and it is on their teachings, expressed through the Guru Granth Sahib (the Scriptures) and the community of believers, that the faith is built.

The Lives and Teachings of the Gurus

Guru Nanak (1469-1539)

Guru Nanak was born into a Hindu family in Talwandi, northern India, in 1469. Due to border changes, Talwandi is now in Pakistan and it has been renamed Nankana Sahib in the Guru's honour.

His father, Mehta Kalu, was an accountant. He was quite well off and Nanak had a happy childhood.

Like other religious leaders, there are stories told about Nanak's birth, suggesting that he would grow up to be someone special.

It is said that when Nanak was born his sister, Nanaki, was waiting outside the room. The midwife came out to speak to her -

Guru Nanak

Mehta Kalu took his daughter into the room to see the addition to the family. The new baby was named Nanak. Soon after his birth his parents asked astrologers to study the stars to find out what sort of life their child would have. They cast the chart –

There are many stories about the young Nanak. Here is one of them:

One day Mehta Kalu sent his son into the nearest town with some money telling him to spend it as wisely as he could. The boy set off with Bala, his best friend. As they journeyed they met some holy men who lived in the forest and Nanak stopped to talk to them. He was fascinated by them and asked lots of questions. He wondered about how they survived with no homes, clothes, food or jobs.

'We don't need these things,' said one of them. 'We eat when God sends us food.'

'And how long is it since you last ate?' asked Nanak.

'Four days,' came the reply.

Nanak and Bala continued their journey but Nanak was very quiet, thinking about the holy men and what they said. When they arrived Nanak started to spend his father's money on food for the holy men. Bala was horrified when he realised what his friend was doing. He knew that Nanak's father would be angry and he tried to talk his friend out of what he was doing. But it made no difference to Nanak.

Laden with the food, Nanak and Bala returned to the forest in search of the holy men who were very grateful to the boys and to God for the food which Nanak had brought.

After they had left the forest Nanak said to his friend, 'What have we done?'.

'We!' said Bala, 'I had nothing to do with this. I tried to stop you but you wouldn't listen!'

Nanak's father was very angry:

At around the age of 30 Nanak had an experience which confirmed for him what God wanted him to do with the rest of his life.

Following his usual custom he went to the river early one morning to bathe and say his prayers. He undressed, left his clothes on the bank and went down into the water. Some time later his friends found his clothes but there was no sign of Nanak.

They feared that Nanak had drowned and started to look for him. Everyone was very worried. However, three days later he reappeared at the very same spot where he had disappeared. His friends were very curious as to what had happened but Nanak said very little about his experience during the days he was missing.

However, it did have a tremendous effect on Nanak, for, at the age of 30, he left the security of his home and family and began to travel around teaching, preaching, and showing by his example what he claimed to be the way of life that was pleasing to God.

During the next 20 years he travelled from place to place, stopping at both Hindu and Muslim holy sites in India and possibly beyond, although the actual route of his travels cannot be identified. During his travels he encouraged others to commit their lives to God. He taught about the oneness of God and the equality of humankind. He taught that his followers should be prepared to work hard in the service of God and of humanity.

Question
- How do these stories show the importance of Guru Nanak to the Sikh faith?

In about 1520 he settled in the village of Kartarpur in the Punjab, where he established the first Sikh community. (The term 'Sikh" comes from a Punjabi word meaning 'to learn'.)

As Guru Nanak's life began to draw to an end, he appointed one of his followers, Lehna (Angad) to be his successor and to continue to care for and teach the Sikh community.

One of his followers was a man called Lehna. He always sought to put the teachings of Guru Nanak into practice. One day he came to visit Guru Nanak in Kartarpur where he had settled. He put on his best clothes in honour of the Guru and set off to the village.

When he had almost reached his destination he came across some villagers who were out in the fields gathering grass into bundles to take into the village for the cows to eat. Just as he was passing by, a large bundle of wet, muddy grass was ready to be taken into the village. Without hesitation Lehna picked up the bundle and carried it into the village. As he carried it both he and his clothes got very wet and muddy. As he entered the village Guru Nanak's wife saw him.

Is this how we Sikhs treat a good man by making him carry the heaviest and dirtiest bundle?

You do not understand. That is not a load of grass, it is a crown to honour the best of men.

This is just one example of the love and devotion which Lehna showed, leading Guru Nanak to choose him as his successor.

Guru Angad (1504-52)

He was born in 1504 in Matte di Sarai in India and became Guru on the death of Guru Nanak in 1539.

Whilst on pilgrimage to a Hindu shrine Lehna met Guru Nanak and became one of his closest followers. The Guru appointed him as his successor and changed his name to 'Angad', which means, 'my limb' or 'part of me'. This change of name stresses the continuity of the Guru's message. Sikhs believe that each of the Gurus is faithful to the same message that Guru Nanak taught.

Angad was a very learned man. He gathered together some of the first Guru's hymns and had these, and some of his own, written down in Gurmukhi. Gurmukhi script is the written form of the Punjabi language. He set up schools to teach young people to read and write Gurmukhi (Punjabi). He also encouraged his followers to take part in sport on a regular basis believing that a sound mind and a healthy body were both pleasing to God. Many gurdwaras still organise sporting events, especially at festival times.

Guru Angad

Guru Amar Das (1479-1574)

Guru Amar Das

The third Guru was born in 1479 and became Guru in 1552 when he was 73 years old. He was a man of great wisdom and devotion to God who did much to encourage the growing number of Sikhs in their faith.

He divided the Punjab into 22 Sikh districts and sent people out to spread the faith. He realised that gathering together in celebrations strengthened faith and the feeling of belonging. He therefore encouraged Sikhs to gather together at his headquarters in Goindwal three times a year. These gatherings took place at the time of three important Hindu festivals and had the effect of encouraging Sikhs to decide between obeying the Guru's call or observing Hindu rituals.

He continued the insistence that Sikhs should be prepared to eat with anyone. This promoted the idea of the langar. This is the kitchen attached to each gurdwara where Sikhs eat together to show hospitality and to express rejection of the idea of social and religious class and caste (see page 44). He made a rule that anyone who wanted to see him must first eat in the langar.

Guru Ram Das (1534-81)

Lahore was the birthplace of Guru Ram Das who was born there in 1534. He was a very humble man who lived his life in the service of others. He died in Goindwal in 1581.

During the period in which he was Guru (1574-81) the Sikh community grew rapidly. He is best remembered for founding the city of Amritsar, which has become a very important centre for Sikhism. He invited people with different trades and business interests to settle in Amritsar (which was originally called Ramdaspur) to found the community (see page 59 for more about Amritsar). He also composed many hymns. One of these, the Lavan, forms an important part of the Sikh wedding ceremony. It is sung while the bridal couple circle the Guru Granth Sahib (see page 82).

Shortly before his death in 1581 his son, Arjan, succeeded him as Guru.

Guru Arjan (1563-1606)

Guru Arjan and the Harimandir (Golden Temple) in Amritsar.

The son of Guru Ram Das, Arjan was born in Goindwal in 1563 and became Guru shortly before the death of his father in 1581. He was the fifth Sikh Guru and its first Guru-martyr.

He completed the building of Amritsar, which had been started by Guru Ram Das, including the Harimandir (the Golden Temple, see page 59). He continued the social reforms and the missionary efforts of the other Gurus, and built other Sikh towns.

Guru Arjan is also famous for collecting the hymns of the first four Gurus, along with some of his own and some from Hindu and Muslim holy men, to produce the Adi Granth, the first version of the Sikh Scriptures. The Adi Granth was kept in the Harimandir in Amritsar.

At this time the Sikhs enjoyed good relations with the Moghal Emperor Akbar, and were allowed to live in peace and worship as they pleased.

However, when Akbar died and was succeeded by Jahangir difficulties arose. Guru Arjan was taken before Jahangir, fined 200,000 rupees and ordered to remove some hymns from the Adi Granth. He refused. Jahangir was angry and Guru Arjan was tortured and killed.

Guru Hargobind (1595-1644)

Guru Hargobind succeeded his father as Guru in 1606 and is sometimes called the Warrior Guru.

After the martyrdom of Guru Arjan he said that instead of wearing prayer beads he would wear two kirpans (swords) - one to stand for spiritual power and the other worldly power. The spiritual power was God's truth as expressed through the message of the Gurus, and worldly power was expressed in standing against oppression and injustice. The two kirpans have become part of the Khanda, a very important Sikh symbol (see page 25). The Guru trained and encouraged his followers to be prepared to fight if necessary.

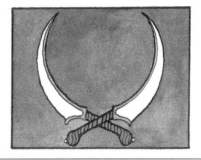

Activity
* Write down the meaning of the two kirpans in your own words.

Guru Har Rai (1630-61)

Guru Har Rai became Guru in 1644 on the death of Guru Hargobind. He continued the military training of the Sikhs that Guru Hargobind had begun.

He is chiefly remembered for setting up a large dispensary at which free medicines were distributed to those who were sick. In India today some of the larger gurdwaras run a free dispensary and offer free medical treatment to those in need.

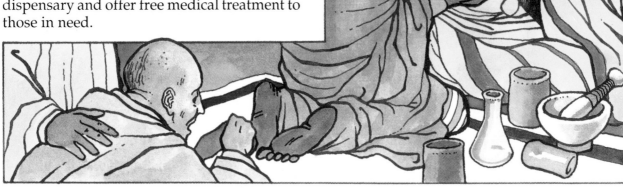

Guru Har Krishan (1656-64)

Guru Har Krishan was a child of only 5 years old when he was installed as the eighth Sikh Guru. He was Guru for only three years when he died in Delhi during a smallpox epidemic. During the epidemic it is reported that a number of people were healed when they drank some spring water given to them by the Guru. There is now a gurdwara built over the site of the spring and people still go to it in the hope of healing.

When he was close to death he told his followers to look for his successor in the village of Bakala.

Guru Har Krishan

Guru Tegh Bahadur (1621-75)

Guru Tegh Bahadur was the youngest son of Guru Hargobind. He became Guru in 1664 at a time of growing persecution of the Sikhs. They were being asked to renounce their faith and if they would not they were forced to pay large taxes and many of their schools and gurdwaras were closed.

Guru Tegh Bahadur believed that everyone should be free to worship God in whatever way they believed to be right, and he led the Sikhs in battle to fight for this right.

He was captured and imprisoned. He and four of his closest followers refused to renounce their faith. They were tortured and killed. He is therefore remembered as the second Guru-martyr.

Question

- Guru Tegh Bahadur and many other Sikhs were killed for their faith. Why do you think people sometimes prefer to die rather than to give up their religion?

Guru Tegh Bahadur was roasted alive, preferring to die rather than renounce his faith.

Guru Gobind Singh (1666-1708)

He was installed as the Sikhs' tenth Guru in 1675 after the martyrdom of Guru Tegh Bahadur.

He is chiefly remembered for two things. Firstly, it was through him that the Khalsa was formed. Secondly, he declared that the line of human Gurus was to come to an end with him.

At Baisakhi in 1699 Guru Gobind Singh called his followers to Anandpur where he happened to be celebrating the festival. From the assembled crowd he used the dedication and trust of five men as an example of how all Sikhs should be prepared to live and die. From this time onwards he encouraged his followers to wear what are now known as the Five Ks (since their names in Punjabi all begin with a 'K' sound). He also said that all Sikh males should take the name 'Singh' (meaning 'Lion') and all females the name 'Kaur' (meaning 'Princess') as a symbol of equality and of belonging to the Khalsa.

Before he died Guru Gobind Singh told his followers that there were to be no more human Gurus. Instead the Sikh Scriptures, which Guru Arjan compiled and which he had revised, were to be their living Guru. In the Guru Granth Sahib they would find all the guidance and inspiration they needed to live as Sikhs.

It was, therefore, with the assassination of Guru Gobind Singh in 1708 that the Sikhs' line of human Gurus came to an end.

Question

- In this painting, Guru Gobind Singh is shown as a powerful military man. Why might this image be important for Sikhs?

The Guru Granth Sahib. Since the death of Guru Gobind Singh, the Sikh scriptures have been the Sikh's guru. It is shown the same respect that would be shown to a human guru.

The Gurus' Importance for Sikhs Today

Events from the lives of the spiritual leaders and founders of every religious tradition are remembered by believers as a way of honouring them and as a way of exploring their significance and teachings. The example they gave has acted, and continues to act as a source of inspiration for believers, as a way of deepening faith, and as an aid to help them in their worship of God.

Remembering events from the lives of their Gurus is important for Sikhs as a source of inspiration, as a guide for living and as a way of helping them to worship God.

Activities

Key Elements

1 Through how many Gurus was the Sikh faith revealed?

2 What was the basis of the message that they gave?

3 What do Sikhs believe to be special about these Gurus?

4 Who was the first Sikh Guru and when did he live?

5 When, with whom, and why did the line of living Gurus come to an end?

6 a) What was the original name of the second Guru?
b) What was it changed to and why?

7 a) How old was Guru Amar Das when he became Guru?
b) What rule did he make about those who wished to see him?

8 Which Guru founded Amritsar?

9 a) What relation was the fifth Guru to Guru Ram Das?
b) How did the fifth Guru die?

10 Which Guru is also known as the Warrior Guru and why?

11 What do the two kirpans (swords) he pledged to wear stand for?

12 What is Guru Har Rai chiefly remembered for?

13 a) How old was the eighth Guru when he was installed?
b) How long was he Guru?

14 What relation was Guru Tegh Bahadur to Guru Hargobind?

15 How did Guru Tegh Bahadur die?

16 For what two things are Guru Gobind Singh chiefly remembered?

17 When and how did Guru Gobind Singh die?

Think About It

18 What is the difference between astrology and astronomy? Why do you think Nanak's parents had an astrological chart cast when he was born?

19 In what ways do you think the lives and teachings of the Gurus affect the way in which Sikhs live their lives today?

20 Why do you think many Sikh homes have pictures of at least one of the Gurus in them?

Assignments

1 Make a chart listing the names of the Sikh Gurus, when they were born, when they became Guru, when they died, and one other thing about them.

2 Write an outline of the life of Guru Nanak and at least two of the other Sikh Gurus. (You can use the information in this chapter as a starting point but you should also try to find out information from elswhere e.g. the class or school library.)

3 Try to find out what Sikhs believe happened to Guru Nanak during the three days he was missing. (See the account of his call on page 14.)

4 Find out about some of the ways in which Sikhs show respect for their Gurus.

3

The Khalsa

- Background
- The Founding of the Khalsa
- Panj Kakke (The Five Ks)

- Nishan Sahib (The Sikh Flag)
- Amrit Sanskar (Initiation into the Khalsa)

Background

From the beginning of the seventeenth century (CE) the Sikh community began to experience persecution:

- Guru Arjan was tortured and killed in 1606.
- Guru Hargobind started to encourage Sikhs to fight for what was right, and protect themselves and the rights of all people, irrespective of race, caste, sex or religion.
- Guru Tegh Bahadur, in response to a request for help from some Hindus who were also being persecuted for their faith, went to Delhi with some of his closest followers to ask the Muslim authorities to cease their persecution and release the people who were imprisoned for refusing to renounce their faith. Guru Tegh Bahadur's plea fell on deaf ears, he and his followers were imprisoned, tortured and killed.
- Guru Gobind Rai then became Guru in 1675 and the persecution continued. Life for Sikhs was very difficult indeed.

The Founding of the Khalsa

In April 1699 Guru Gobind Rai called his followers together at Anandpur to celebrate Baisakhi (see page 67). A large crowd gathered and the Guru, with a drawn sword in his hand, called for volunteers who were prepared to die for their faith. After an awkward silence one man stepped forward rather hesitantly and followed the Guru into his tent. A short while later the Guru emerged from the tent with his bloodstained sword. He repeated his call. Eventually five people had followed the Guru into his tent, each offering their lives for their faith. The crowd was stunned and silent.

The Guru went back inside his tent and led out the five men unharmed. These men, remembered as the **Panj Piare** ('the faithful and beloved ones'), are looked up to as examples of people who were prepared to put their life at risk in order to be obedient to the call of their Guru and the demands of their faith.

Guru Gobind Rai then made a nectar by dissolving sugar crystals in water and stirring it with a two edged sword (a khanda). He sprinkled this over the Panj Piare and they drank some. They made some solemn vows of commitment. Through this initiation ceremony they became the first members of the Khalsa.

Guru Gobind Singh with the Panj Piare.

The Panj Piare

The names of the five brave followers who offered their lives to their Guru and for their faith are:

- **Daya Ram**, a Kshatriya, a member of the traditional ruling, warrior caste;
- **Dharam Das**, a jat, a member of the group whose traditional occupation was farming, from Delhi;
- **Mukham Chand**, a low-caste washerman, from the district of Gujarat;
- **Sahib Chand**, a baker from Biharr;
- **Himmat Rai**, a potter from Jagganath.

They came from different castes and different places, yet they had in common a commitment to their faith. They are remembered for their example of faithfulness and dedication, for their willingness to offer everything in response to the call and demands of faith. Sikhs aim to follow their example.

As a symbol of having become equal, now they were members of the Khalsa, the Guru said that all males should take the name '**Singh**' (meaning 'lion') and all females the name '**Kaur**' (meaning 'princess'). He became Guru Gobind Singh and his wife Mata Sahib Kaur. This was a very important action since, for their Hindu neighbours, the 'gotra' (kinship-group or caste) of a person was identifiable through their name. This meant that Sikhs were not to be identified by where they came from, or the position they held in society, but by their membership of the Khalsa.

In addition to this, Sikhs began to wear five symbols of their faith (Panj Kakke, the Five Ks) to display their dedication to, and membership of, the Khalsa.

The formation of the Khalsa at Baisakhi in 1699 helped members of the Sikh faith to come to terms with, and overcome, the persecution they were suffering. It helped them to identify with their religion and with each other, fostering a sense of identity and belonging; it continues to do the same today.

Vows taken when becoming members of the Khalsa:

- wear the Panj Kakke (the Five Ks) - see pages 24 and 25;
- not to take drugs and intoxicants;
- respect women (no adultery or rape - the violation of women was and remains a common act in war - Sikhs although engaged in battle at the time were to have higher standards);
- not to eat meat which had been ritually slaughtered;
- follow the teachings of the Guru;
- serve the Guru, with arms if necessary;
- reject all caste differences - all Khalsa members should be regarded as brothers and sisters.

Question

- How would you have reacted if you were in the crowd at Baisakhi in 1699, when the Guru came out and asked for another volunteer?

The Panj Kakke

Wearing the Panj Kakke or Five Ks is important to the majority of Sikhs, both male and female. They are symbols of belonging to the Khalsa, of being a Sikh. They are a link with an important event in Sikh history. They are a physical way in which a person is able to show their obedience to the teachings of their Gurus. They also reflect what Sikh teaching is about; the way that you should live your life.

Kesh

This boy is having his turban tied. Under it, his hair will remain uncut.

Kesh (uncut hair) is a symbol of a Sikh's devotion to God. It is a symbol of the spirituality which lies at the heart of the Sikh religion. The turban is not one of the Five Ks but is worn to cover the uncut hair. It is mainly worn by men but some women may also wear it.

Kangha

It is important to keep the hair clean and tidy. A kangha (comb) is used to do this. It may also be used to keep the hair in place under the turban. It symbolises the discipline needed to control and develop the spiritual side of one's nature and faith.

Kara

The kara is a steel bangle worn on the right wrist. Originally a broader version of it may have been worn to protect the sword arm in battle. It is a symbol of the unity and equality of the Khalsa, since all may wear it and it is affordable by all. Being a circle, which has no beginning and no end, it can be a constant reminder to the wearer of the eternal nature of God. It also acts as a symbol of the bond which exists between all who wear it and between those who wear it and God.

Kirpan

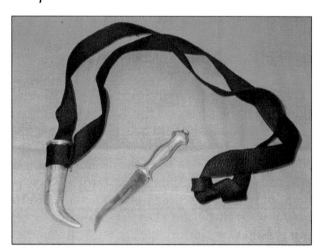

The kirpan (sword) is symbolic of both the power and the freedom to be found within the faith. At the time of the formation of the Khalsa it was used in battle but today it stands as a symbol of the spiritual warfare in which all members of the Khalsa are engaged.

Question

- Imagine you are a Sikh and someone, seeing your kirpan, accuses you of carrying a dangerous weapon. How would you reply?

Kachera

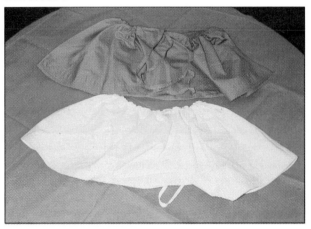

Kachera are under-shorts worn by both men and women. Sikhs originally wore them as clothes suitable for going into battle. When the Khalsa was formed many Hindu holy men in northern India wore rather long, flowing cloaks which were impractical for going into battle. By wearing the kachera, Sikhs were showing that they were prepared to take up arms to defend their religion and the right of others to practice without fear of persecution. Since they are a modest form of dress, they have also come to symbolise the idea of modesty and of living a good life.

Fact Box

Some Sikhs choose not to wear all of these symbols. For example, in Britain today some Sikh men are cutting their hair and shaving their beards. Some may choose only to wear the kara. Nevertheless, for many within the Sikh community, these symbols remain an important way of expressing their belonging to the faith, their unity with each other and their identity as Sikhs.

Question

- Why do you think some Sikhs in Britain and other Western countries decide not to wear all 5 of the 'K's?
- What things influence the way you dress?

Nishan Sahib

An important Sikh symbol is the Nishan Sahib, the flag which flies outside each and every Sikh gurdwara (place of worship). This too has a link with Baisakhi as the Nishan Sahib is replaced each year during the celebration of that festival.

The Nishan Sahib has the Khanda on a saffron (yellow) background. The Khanda is also found elsewhere, both inside and outside the gurdwara and in many Sikh homes. Some Sikh car drivers also display the symbol in their cars.

The Nishan Sahib, with the Khanda symbol.

The Khanda takes its name from its central symbol, a double-edged sword used in many Sikh ceremonies. The chakra (circle) which has no beginning and no end shows the eternal nature of God and limits the area within it - a sign that Sikhs should always try to live within God's rule. The two kirpans represent the call upon Sikhs to defend the truth.

Activity

- Write down in your own words the meaning of the symbols which make up the Khanda. Then say why you think the Khanda is so important for Sikhs.

Amrit Sanskar

This painting shows Guru Gobind Singh performing the first Amrit Sanskar ceremony. In the background are the Panj Piare.

Membership of the Khalsa is an important aspect of being a Sikh, yet not all Sikhs have been initiated into it. A child born to a Sikh family and brought up in accordance with Sikh tradition is regarded as a Sikh. Initiation into the Khalsa is seen as a personal commitment which individuals make when they feel able to carry out the responsibilities of their faith. A convert from another religion is initiated into the Khalsa in the same way as someone who has been born into a Sikh family.

The ceremony of initiation (Amrit Sanskar) can take place at any time but quite often Baisakhi is chosen, due to its links with the foundation of the Khalsa. The ceremony usually takes place in the gurdwara but it can take place anywhere so long as it is in the presence of the Guru Granth Sahib.

Five respected members of the Khalsa, representing the Panj Piare (see page 22f) conduct the ceremony in front of the Guru Granth Sahib. Those who wish to become Khalsa members have the basic principles of the faith explained to them and are asked if they accept them. After they agree to this, prayers are offered for the amrit preparation and a section of the Guru Granth Sahib is read out.

The amrit is then prepared. Amrit is the mixture of water and sugar crystals mixed together in a steel bowl (called a bata) and stirred by each of the five conducting the ceremony using a khanda (a double-edged sword). Each of the five holds the bata with the left hand and takes it in turn to stir the mixture with the khanda using the right hand. While this is taking place they recite five compositions by the Gurus contained in the Scriptures. The five compositions are the Japji of Guru Nanak, the Jap, Swayyas and Chaupai of Guru Gobind Singh and the Anand of Guru Amar Das. The five conducting the ceremony sit in a special position called the bir asan - the right knee must be on the ground and the left must be raised.

When the amrit is ready another prayer is said and those who are to be initiated are called to sit in the bir asan position in order to receive the amrit into their cupped hands to drink. They recite the words 'Raheguru ji ka Khalsa, raheguru ji ki fateh' (the Khalsa is of God, the victory is God's). This is repeated five times in all.

Following this the amrit is sprinkled five times into the eyes and hair of those to be initiated. They then stand and each, in turn, takes a sip of the amrit from the bata. The Mool Mantra, the first words of the Guru Granth Sahib are recited a number of times before one of the five tells the new members their future responsibilities as members of the Khalsa. A final lesson from the Scriptures is read and all those present share the karah parshad (see page 28).

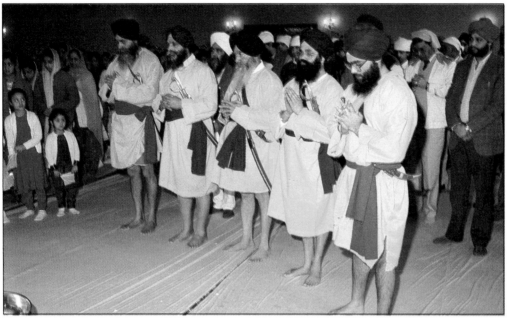

This photograph shows five Sikhs in full ceremonial dress. They are wearing the 5 Ks and represent the Panj Piares at the original celebration of Amrit Sanskar. Although non-Sikhs may think such dress is usual, it is important, for it represents many of the central values of the Sikh faith.

Karah Parshad

Karah parshad is served at the end of all Sikh services and ceremonies. It is made of flour (or semolina), ghee (clarified butter) and sugar.

Distributing karah parshad.

If you would like to try karah parshad, here is a recipe:

Ingredients (in roughly equal proportions)
- Semolina (or flour), from a packet not a tin
- Sugar (brown is best)
- Ghee (clarified butter, although any will do)
- Water

Method
Melt the ghee (or butter) over a low heat, add the semolina (or flour) and cook gently for about five minutes.

Dissolve the sugar in some warm water and add this gradually to the mixture. Cook, stirring all the time, until it leaves the side of the pan.

Allow to cool slightly. Divide into small portions and eat while it is still warm.

Activities

Key Elements

1 Look at the Punjabi words in this chapter. Try to explain what each of them means to someone who has never come across them before?

2 When and by whom was the Khalsa founded?

3 Who were the Panj Piare? Give an example of when and how they are remembered by Sikhs today.

4 Explain why Sikh men take the name 'Singh' and Sikh women the name 'Kaur'.

5 a) Draw the Panj Kakke (or Five Ks) as they appear on pages 24 and 25. Label each one with both its Punjabi name and the English translation.
b) Explain the symbolism of each of the Panj Kakke.

6 a) Where might you find the symbol known as the Khanda?
b) From which part of the symbol does the Khanda take its name?

Think About It

7 What do you think happened inside the tent between the Panj Piare and Guru Gobind Rai at Baisakhi in 1699?

8 How might Sikhs feel as they commit themselves during the Amrit Sanskar ceremony? What difference might it make to their daily lives?

9 Why do you think it is important to many Sikhs to wear the Panj Kakke? Think about some of the advantages and disadvantages of wearing them in Britain today.

Assignment

1 Make detailed notes on the following: the foundation of the Khalsa; the Panj Kakke; the Amrit Sanskar ceremony.

4

The Guru Granth Sahib

- The Adi Granth
- The Guru Granth Sahib
- Gurmukhi Script

- Extracts from the Guru Granth Sahib
- The Dasam Granth

This photograph shows the Guru Granth Sahib, covered by beautiful cloths (called *romallas*), in the Harimandir (the Golden Temple) at Amritsar. (Some of the features shown here will be explained in the chapter on Sikh worship.)

When Sikhs first gathered together there was no special place of worship for them: they simply met together in the presence of the Guru. The Guru Granth Sahib became the living Guru to Sikhs on the death of Guru Gobind Singh. Thus, all Sikh services and ceremonies must take place in the presence of the Guru Granth Sahib. It is treated with the greatest respect and honour. It is read regularly and its teachings listened to and put into practice in the daily life of the believer.

The Sikh Scriptures bring together the words of a number of Sikh Gurus, along with those of some other holy men.

The Adi Granth

The first completed version of the Sikh Scriptures, the Adi Granth, is attributed to Guru Arjan, who drew together the teachings of his predecessors, his own teachings and those of other holy men, in 1604 CE. Shortly after its completion the Adi Granth was placed in the newly built Harimandir in Amritsar. (The original Adi Granth can be seen, carefully preserved, in the gurdwara Shish Mahal in Kartarpur.)

Installing the Adi Granth in the Harimandir in Amritsar was an important landmark in the development of the Sikh faith. By having a central collection of the Scriptures available for public reading it provided a bench mark by which other copies could be checked and so encouraged consistency in copying and teaching. It also gave Sikhs the framework for their daily life and so helped to reinforce their identity. The treatment of the Adi Granth in the Harimandir set the structure of Sikh worship which remains the same today.

In 1704 CE Guru Gobind Singh, extended the Adi Granth by adding some hymns or shabads from his father and immediate predecessor, Guru Teg Bahadur. It is this extended version of the original Adi Granth, the Guru Granth Sahib, which is the focus of attention in congregational worship in the gurdwara today.

The Guru Granth Sahib

The Guru Granth Sahib (or Adi Granth as it is also called) has 1,430 pages. It contains 5,894 shabads or hymns arranged into 31 ragas or musical groupings. Each copy, regardless of its size, is identical in the way in which the pages are laid out. This means, for example, that passages will always appear on the same page and will begin and end in the same place. 'AG 1276: Guru Nanak' means that this particular shabad by Guru Nanak will always be found on page number 1276 of the Holy Granth.

This photograph shows the Guru Granth Sahib being carried on the head of a Sikh in the Harimandir (the Golden Temple) in Amritsar. It is a sign of the great respect in which this holy book is held.

Question

- Look again at these two photographs. What do they suggest to you about the way Sikhs regard the Guru Granth Sahib?

Language and Script

The Guru Granth Sahib is written in Gurmukhi, the written form of Punjabi (see page 32f). It literally means 'from the Guru's mouth' pointing to the traditional Sikh belief that the Scriptures contain the actual words and verses spoken by their Gurus. Translations of the Guru Granth Sahib have been made into other languages (e.g. Hindi, Urdu, English, French) but these are not used as a basis for worship.

Gurmukhi Script

These handwritten Shabads (verses) in Gurmukhi script are from the 'Bani', or sacred songs, of Bhagat Kabir. Some of Kabir's songs are included in the Guru Granth Sahib.

The Punjabi language is a major language of the Indian subcontinent. The written form of this language is Gurmukhi.

The alphabet consists of 35 letters (characters), written on the page from left to right. It is arranged in seven groupings of five letters each, mostly based on phonetic sound patterns.

Research Question
- Use a dictionary to find out what the word phonetic means.

The first three letters of the alphabet are the equivalent to the five English vowels. In addition to these there are another nine vowel signs.

When one language is translated into another there is not always an equivalent letter or sound. This can lead to different, and sometimes misleading, spellings of words. In this publication spellings of Punjabi words translated into English have been based on a glossary which has been produced

by the School Curriculum and Assessment Authority in consultation with members of different faith traditions.

Transliteration: the process of matching letters or characters in one alphabet with those of a different alphabet.

Activity

- Once you have looked through the letters and their English equivalents, copy out the Mool Mantra on page 36 and beneath each of the Punjabi letters write down how it should sound. Then try to read out the Mool Mantra in Punjabi.

Contents

The Holy Granth is unique among the sacred writings of religious traditions in that it contains material from people who themselves do not belong to that tradition. There are writings from Muslims and Hindus. This material is nevertheless regarded as sacred, showing the respect and tolerance which Sikhs are expected to demonstrate towards others. It also reflects the belief that truth is not the monopoly of any one religious tradition and that the love and grace of God is for all.

> *The four castes of Kshatriyas, Brahmins, Shudras and Vaishyas are equal partners in divine instruction. Nanak, he who dwells on the name of God alone is emancipated in this age.*
> *AdiGranth 747: Guru Arjan*

The length of a shabad varies; some are just a few lines others run to several pages. A small portion at the beginning and the end of the Guru Granth Sahib is meant to be recited and forms the devotional readings for the morning and evening prayers. The other contents are meant to be sung and so the shabads are not arranged by subject or author but rather in the order (ragas) in which they are to be sung.

The Guru Granth Sahib's opening passage is known as the **Mool Mantra**. The passage which Sikhs believe comes from the lips of Guru Nanak himself emphasises belief in one eternal, creator God, Akal Purakh. Sikhs are expected to recite it daily. It is also used to mark the beginning and end of each of the 31 ragas.

The Mool Mantra makes some important statements about God: God is eternal, that is, beyond time, without beginning and without end; God is perfect and does not have such imperfect characteristics as hatred or fear for example; God can be known through revelation.

Guru Arjan established the framework for the order in which the shabads were to be arranged. Guru Gobind Singh followed this order and added the later works using the same framework. Under each raga the shabads of the Gurus are arranged in the order of their succession. Next come the shabads of other holy men, starting with Muslims and including Hindus from both low and high castes.

The number of shabads originating from Guru Arjan is the greatest (2,218), next is Guru Nanak (974) and then Guru Amar Das (907). Some have a relatively small number of shabads included in the Guru Granth Sahib (e.g. Farid, a Muslim writer, 116) and therefore are not represented in each raga.

The Mool Mantra in Gurmukhi, with English translation.

Treatment

The Guru Granth Sahib was not printed until the nineteenth century and there was resistance from some within the faith community. They had a genuine fear that by printing the Holy Granth more copies would be available, and some pople would not know how to treat it with the respect it deserved. At the very least, hands should be washed and some Sikhs take a bath before touching the Scriptures. With the printing of the Guru Granth Sahib its length was standardised to 1430 pages.

Teachings

The teachings contained in the Guru Granth Sahib provide a framework by which Sikhs should live their lives in a good and meaningful way, mindful of responsibilities towards God, other members of their faith community and the whole of humanity.

The Guru Granth Sahib in its revelation of Akal Purakh encourages belief in one God (monotheism). There are a number of names used for God, each emphasising different aspects of belief about, and the character of, God. **Akal Purakh** meaning 'the Eternal One' or 'the Timeless One' was used by Guru Nanak and so appears frequently in the Guru Granth Sahib. **Sat Guru** meaning 'the True Guru' and **Raheguru**, 'Wonderful Lord' are also used. Prayer, meditation and worship should be based on the revelation of God and the teachings of the Gurus as contained in the Holy Granth. Idolatry in any form is condemned.

The Guru Granth Sahib encourages marriage and family life as an honourable way of living, designed to provide mutual support in following the teachings of the Gurus. It is important to work hard and be generous towards those less fortunate than yourself. Discrimination of any sort is condemned and the equality of all in the eyes of Akal Purakh is emphasised within the Guru Granth Sahib.

Sikhs are called upon to put these teachings into practice in every aspect of their daily lives. The Guru Granth Sahib is therefore of central importance to the life, work and worship of the Sikh community.

Worship

Both men and women may read from the Guru Granth Sahib during worship.

The Guru Granth Sahib is central in the public worship of Sikhs and is thus central to the layout of the gurdwara. It forms the focal point of all Sikh services and ceremonies (see Chapters 6 and 8).

Question
- Explain in your own words what is meant by the sentence which says, 'It forms the focal point of all Sikh ceremonies and services.'

It is not unusual for a copy of the Guru Granth Sahib to be taken from the gurdwara into a new home or a new business in order for a continual reading (an **Akand Path**) to take place. Sikhs believe that by doing this they will receive the blessing of Akal Purakh.

Blessing a new home

When we moved into our new house three years ago my parents arranged to have the Holy Granth come to bless us in our home. We moved in and unpacked everything. It took quite a long time for us to do that. My sister and I share a room and we didn't have enough space for everything so we had to sort some things out to go in the loft out of the way.

A few weeks after we had moved in Mum and Dad said that we had to get the house ready to receive the Guru Granth Sahib. The day before we had to move the furniture out of the front room to make space for it and for our friends and relatives. We cleaned the carpet, wiped down all the paint and cleaned the windows. Mum, my elder brother and younger sister came back from the shops with lots of food for the meal afterwards and flowers to go into the room and on the doorstep of the house. The kitchen was cleaned as was the hallway. We spent a lot of time getting food ready.

Some men from our gurdwara arrived carrying the Guru Granth Sahib. We were watching for them coming and opened the door to greet them. We bowed low as the Guru Granth Sahib came into our house and my sister dropped flower petals in the hall which the men walked on as it was carried into the front room. Some of the adults were singing hymns but the children just watched.

Once in the room the granthi opened the Holy Book and began to read from it. It was a special message for us and a blessing on our new home. The singing continued for quite a while and friends and relatives came to join us. Our next door neighbours came too but they were a bit lost because they don't understand Punjabi. Afterwards we ate the food in the kitchen and in the garden.

Translations of some words from the Guru Granth Sahib

Know all human beings to be repositories of Divine Light;
Stop not to inquire about their caste;
In the hereafter there are no castes.

O shrewd businessman, do only profitable business; Deal only in that commodity which shall accompany you after death.

After you shall depart this life, God shall demand a reckoning of your deeds that in his ledger are recorded.

Says Nanak, 'Falsehood must be destroyed; Truth in the end shall prevail.'

Under the shelter of the Supreme Being, not a whiff of hot air touches us. All around us is drawn the mystic circle of divine protection ... Says Nanak, 'In his grace has the Lord come to succor us.'

Of all prayers of the heart, the best prayer is the prayer to the Master to be given the grace of properly praising the Lord.

Contemplate solely on the Name of God - fruitless are all other rituals.
Contemplate the Name yourself; inspire it to others;
By attending to it, discoursing of it, living by it, obtain liberation.

Heaven is not attained without good deeds.

One who claims to be a saint,
And goes about begging -
Do not touch his feet!
He whose livelihood is earned through work,
And part given away in charity -
Such a one, Nanak, truly knows the way of God.

Why do you go to the forest in search of God?
He lives in all and is yet ever distinct;
He abides with you, too,
As fragrance dwells in a flower,
And reflection in a mirror;
So does God dwell inside everything;
Seek him, therefore, in your heart.

This earth is a garden,
The Lord its gardener,
Cherishing all, none neglected.

Question

* The words of the Guru Granth Sahib offer comfort and strength to many Sikhs. From what or whom do you draw strength?

The Dasam Granth 'The Book of the Tenth Master'

Guru Gobind Singh, despite being a great writer and poet, did not include any of his own work in his extension of the Adi Granth.

Bhai Mani Singh, a follower of Guru Gobind Singh, drew this material together and published it in 1734 CE, 26 years after the death of the tenth Guru, naming it **Dasam Granth**.

Just as copies of the Guru Granth Sahib are identical in format so too are copies of the Dasam Granth. It contains a wide range of teaching from Guru Gobind Singh and is highly honoured by Sikhs. However, it is not treated in the same way as the Guru Granth Sahib. The 'Jap' or 'Meditation' is used as part of the daily prayers for Sikhs and along with the Swayyas and Chaupai form part of the recitations which are used during the Amrit Sanskar (see page 30).

> God has no mark or symbols, no colour or caste, not even family lineage; God's form, colour, shape and dress can be described by no one. God is immovable and self-existent and shines in no borrowed light. No one can measure God's might.
>
> *A translation of the opening words of the Jap Sahib.*

Questions
- What impression (picture) of God does the Jap Sahib give?
- What do you believe about God?

The first dictation of the Adi Granth

Two tents were pitched side by side; Guru Arjan was in one of them. He had with him a collection of all the available recorded utterances of the previous four Gurus, his own and those of other spiritual and holy men, both of his day and the past. He prayed and meditated on these and some others were revealed to him by Akal Purakh at this time. He grouped all these together into ragas according to the rhythm of the verses. He then dictated them to the person in the other tent, Bhai Gurdas, who was a learned man and follower of the Guru.

Dictating the Guru Granth Sahib

Guru Gobind Singh set up tents for the dictation just as Guru Arjan had done. He added to the original Adi Granth with the sayings of his father and immediate predecessor, Guru Tegh Bahadur. He did not, however, add any of his own words to the Holy Granth. Thirty years later some of his sayings were gathered together to form the Dasam Granth (see above).

The act of dictation of the Holy Granth by Guru Arjan and later by Guru Gobind Singh is important. It points towards the Sikh belief that the words are those of the Gurus themselves revealing the way to God and the framework by which to live their lives. Hearing those words brings blessing and peace.

The Gutka

Despite the centrality and importance of the Guru Granth Sahib to the Sikh tradition many Sikhs do not have their own copy of the Holy Granth. Precisely because of its importance and the respect with which the Scriptures need to be treated. Among other things, the Guru Granth Sahib should have a separate room of its own especially laid out; many Sikh homes do not have the physical space to house a copy of the Scriptures.

Rather than having a copy of the Guru Granth Sahib in their homes many Sikhs have a copy of the Gutka - a collection of less than twenty of the shabads contained in the Guru Granth Sahib. It is the Gutka which they use for their personal devotions. Sikhs often know passages from the Holy Granth off by heart as they will have heard them sung many times in the gurdwara.

Activities

Key Elements

1 a) What is the Adi Granth?

  b) When and by whom was it first compiled and where is it now?

2 Who extended the first Adi Granth and how did he do this?

3 a) What is the name given to the Sikh Scriptures which form the focal point for Sikh life and worship?
   b) What does its name mean?

4 In what language is the Sikh Scriptures written?

5 What is the Mool Mantra?

6 a) What is the name given to the hymns in the Sikh Scriptures?
   b) How many hymns are there in the Sikh Scriptures?
   c) How are these hymns arranged?
   d) How many of these musical groupings are there?

7 What is the Dasam Granth?

8 What is a Gutka?

Think About It

9 Guru Gobind Singh dictated the Guru Granth Sahib to Bhai Mani Singh using a similar method to the one used by Guru Arjan to dictate the Adi Granth to Bhai Gurdas. Why do you think he did this?

10 Why do you think Sikhs show such great respect to the Guru Granth Sahib?

Assignments

1 Research, and make a list of the different ways in which Sikhs show respect to the Guru Granth Sahib.

2 Choose any three of the quotations on page 38, translated into English from the Sikh Scriptures.
   a) Write out the three quotations you have chosen.

b) How might these words affect the way a Sikh lives?
c) Write out your understanding of these quotations.
d) Share your thoughts with others in your group.
e) In the light of your discussions, make any additions or alterations to what you have written down.

5

Beliefs and Values

- One God
- Human Life and Destiny
- Service to Others

- Equality
- Beliefs and Values in Everyday Life
- Attitudes Towards Some Moral Issues

The Sikh way of life is based on certain beliefs about God, about the world and about humanity. Worship, festivals, ceremonies, the way in which the family is organised, the role of the sexes, diet, work and leisure, attitudes towards people of different faiths are all affected by the basic Sikh beliefs.

One God

Belief in one God is central to the Sikh faith. God is the one eternal, timeless being, the one alone who should be worshipped. God is without beginning or end. God created the world and all that is in it, humankind is the crown of that creation.

Sikhs believe that God created countless universes. They also believe that creation evolved slowly – from air came water, from water the lower forms of life, which led to the development of plants, fish, birds and animals. This then led to the creation of human beings, the highest form of created life on earth.

God is both **sargun** (immanent – everywhere and in everything) and **nirgun** (transcendent – above and beyond creation). The Sikh faith teaches that God never assumes any physical form, either human or animal. For this reason images of God are not to be worshipped since they are the work of human hands and not God. Although God never assumes any physical form he is not distant from those who worship him. God is personal, directly available to everyone and anyone.

As God is everywhere and in everything, God is also above and beyond creation, so God is above and beyond gender, being neither male nor female.

Sikhs believe that this one God is not exclusive to any one religion and that no one religion can claim a monopoly on the truth. Different religions are different routes by which people are led to the same Reality.

Unknowable, infinite,
unapproachable and imperceptible is my Lord.
Not subject to death and destiny,
Casteless.
Unborn, self-illuminated and without desire and doubt.
God has no form, no colour and no features and is revealed only through the True Word.
God has neither father, mother, wife, children, or any other kin.
You, O Lord, are without ancestry, immaculate, transcendent and infinite.
Your light pervades all.

Adi Granth 597

The True One is not far from us, but resides within us.

Adi Granth 421

You are Father, Mother, Friend, Brother,
With you as Succorer in all places, what fear can I have?

Adi Granth 103.

Names for God

The Sikh Gurus recognised that many terms could be used to address God and yet all were inadequate to express in full the reality of God. The Jap of Guru Gobind Singh contains over nine hundred names and references to God which bring out many of God's attributes and character.

These phrases were popular with the Gurus when addressing God:
- *Sat Nam* – the Eternal Reality
- *Akal Purakh* – the Eternal One
- *Raheguru* – Wonderful Lord.

Every section of the Guru Granth Sahib begins with the Mool Mantra (see page 34) which expresses the basis of what Sikhs believe about God. It states that there is one God, who is eternal truth, the creator, who has no fear or enmity, is timeless, immanent, beyond the cycle of birth and death, self-existent, and made known by the grace of the Guru.

Sikhs frequently recite the Mool Mantra in both their public and private worship.

The opening letters of the Mool Mantra form the Ik Onkar symbol, which can be seen in Sikh gurdwaras and homes.

The most important activity for Sikhs is calling to mind, and keeping in mind, the divine name. It is this which deepens a person's spirituality and their faith and helps them to live their life within the community in a way which is pleasing to God.

Human Life and Destiny

Guru Nanak taught that ultimately everything which happens is within the will of God and that people should live their lives in obedience to God's will.

> The word Sikhs use to express the idea of God's Will is **Hukam**.
>
> Sometimes they end an act of worship by reading a short passage taken at random from the Guru Granth Sahib. This too is called 'Hukam' – because God, who controls everything, will use the occasion to make his will known.

The Soul

The Sikh faith teaches that there is a 'divine spark' in each and every individual. The human soul is part of God and is re-absorbed into God on reaching liberation from the cycle of births and deaths.

Sikhs believe that the soul lives through many different forms of existence before being born into a human body. The Gurus taught that there were 84 lakhs of rebirth, which means that there are 8,400,000 forms of life, an immeasurable number. This does not mean that everyone must go through this number of lives before entering the world as a human being. Rather, it points to the vastness of God's creation and to the consequent importance of human life.

Only humans can distinguish between what is right and what is wrong and make moral choices. Human life is therefore the highest form of life on earth and consequently it is at this time that the cycle can potentially be broken. It is **karma**, (actions and their consequences) which determines whether or not a person will achieve liberation from birth and death and so achieve union with God, which is the purpose of human existence. Liberation from the cycle of birth and death is known as **mukti**.

Barriers which block the path to mukti include:

- **maya**: illusion, a materialistic view of the world which leads to ignorance of the will of God;

- **manmukh**: self-centredness instead of God-centredness;

- **kam**: lust;

- **karodh**: anger;

- **lobh**: greed;

- **moh**: worldly attachment;

- **hankar**: pride.

A person should, in this present life, meditate upon God's name, setting heart and mind on God. Such a person will become less self-centred (**manmukh**) and more God-centred (**gurmukh**) and will live their lives in the selfless service of others (**sewa**).

Service to Others

Remembering the name of God (Nam Simran) is central to the Sikh faith and way of life, but it should be combined with service to others. True Sikhs combine both in their daily lives. The following extracts from the Guru Granth Sahib emphasise this point:

True worship consists in the meditation of God's name.

There can be no worship without performing good deeds.

The Sikh way of life is a life of service to God, to the Khalsa and to humanity in general.

There are three distinctive, yet related aspects of sewa.

- **Tan** (Physical) - service to the community. For example, working in the langar, or helping to build and physically maintain the gurdwara.

- **Man** (Mental) - service to the Guru. For example by studying and helping others to understand the teaching of the Gurus expressed through the Guru Granth Sahib.

- **Dhan** (Material) - service to humanity. For example, by giving money to charitable causes, and by giving your time to help people in need.

You should not do these things for your own gain but from a desire to serve in a God-centred way.

Equality

An underlying and determining influence on the Sikh way of life is belief in the oneness of humanity, which leads to an emphasis on the equality of all, male and female, young and old, rich and poor.

Anyone is welcome to eat at the langar.

When the Gurus spoke about the equality of all, they did so within a social situation where a person's role in life was very much determined by the family group or caste into which they had been born. The Gurus rejected treating anyone as inferior or superior on the grounds of caste. The **langar** was, and remains, a very powerful expression of the Gurus' teaching. All are welcome to eat together, irrespective of age, wealth, sex or social standing.

Another symbol of equality are the names 'Singh' and 'Kaur', used by Sikh men and women. Those who share the same name have the same status.

The Gurus also emphasised equality between the sexes. Both men and women are able to lead worship and take an equal part in all religious affairs. The Amrit Sanskar (initiation ceremony) is the same for both men and women.

This emphasis on equality has had two major influences on Sikh life and attitudes towards women and marriage. Firstly, child marriage, a common practice at the time of the Gurus, was banned. In the Punjab today a girl may not marry until she is 18 and a boy until he is 20. Secondly, Sikh widows are allowed to remarry, contrary to the custom of Hindu widows, who, at that time, were expected to throw themselves onto their husband's funeral pyre.

The ideal of equality is not always lived out in practice. For example, some Sikh women feel that they are not given as much influence or responsibility as they would like within community affairs. There is still a tendency to marry within traditional occupational groups. Nevertheless, the Gurus' teaching about equality has, and continues to play, an important part in the life and attitudes of the Sikh community.

Activities

Key Elements

1 Using this chapter as a basis, make a summary of what the Sikh faith teaches about God. (You may like to research this further using other resources.)

2 What do the Punjabi words, 'sargun' and 'nirgun' mean? Explain them in your own words.

3 What do Sikhs believe about humanity?

4 Explain in your own words the meaning of 'karma' and 'mukti'.

5 Within the Sikh faith what is the difference between being 'manmukh' and 'gurmukh'?

6 What is 'sewa'?

7 Outline some of the ways in which the Gurus' teachings on equality are put into practice by Sikhs today.

Think About It

8 a) Read the Mool Mantra. What impression of God does it give?
b) Why do you think it is such an important passage for Sikhs?

9 Discuss the question 'Is there a God?' Give reasons for your opinion and listen to other people's opinions.

10 a) What do you think about the Sikh belief in karma and mukti?
b) Find out what other faith traditions teach about the human soul and about what happens to that soul after a person dies.
c) Discuss the similarities and differences between these beliefs.
d) What do you think?

11 a) As a class, brainstorm the word 'equality'.
b) In groups, using the brainstorm as a starting point for your discussions, think about what equality is and how it is (or is not) worked out in practice today.

Beliefs and Values in Everyday Life

Within the Sikh dharam there is no division between the sacred and the secular. Worship, relationships, work, values and attitudes - all of these are part of a total approach to life and living which has devotion to God at its heart. Of course, there are some Sikhs, just as there are members of other faith traditions, who do not practise their faith to any great extent, if at all, and there are others who are totally devoted to it. The majority of people are somewhere between those two positions.

The Gurus taught that life should be lived in three dimensions and that all three are of equal importance. These three dimensions are:

- **Nam Japna** – to remember God, meditation on the name of God;

- **Kirat Karna** – to earn one's living by honest means;

- **Vand Chhakna** – charitable sharing, of time talents and earnings, with those less fortunate than oneself.

These ensure that for Sikhs the 'religious' or 'spiritual' aspects of life should not, indeed cannot, be divided from the way in which they live their lives, earn their living and use their money; in other words, from the whole of life. They set out for Sikhs a way of life in which prayer/meditation, hard work and generosity are to be regarded as the norm.

The Panj Kakke or Five Ks (see pages 24f) are constant reminders of being Sikh and what that involves. Some Sikhs, particularly in the West, have decided not to wear all of the Panj Kakke, some have cut their hair, for example, and only wear the kara. Whilst still being regarded as Sikhs, many feel that, because the Guru initiated the wearing of them and because wearing them is one of the vows taken at initiation, this is a practise which should not be encouraged.

The primary human duty is to God, expressed through remembering and meditating on the name of God - the first of the three principles outlined above. Here we will examine in more detail the other two principles in relation to the effect on lifestyles and attitudes.

Honest Work (Kirat Karna)

Kirat Karna places on Sikhs an obligation to earn a living by honest means. Sikhs believe that work is a necessity, both for the good of the individual's family, and for society in general. It provides for basic needs such as food, clothing and housing. The form of work (be it manual, professional, agricultural or social) is not of prime importance; but it should not involve deceit, or any other form of underhanded dealing, or exploit other people. Immoral or illegal work is frowned upon. Making a living, for example, by producing harmful drugs or promoting pornography or prostitution is not regarded as earning a living by honest means.

You should earn a living by honest means, and in a way that reflects the values of the Sikh community.

Sikhs believe that wealth in itself is not wrong providing it is gained honestly but to become obsessed by wealth is. The wealth created by hard work should be used for the benefit of the family, the Khalsa and humanity in general.

Generosity (Vand Chhakna)

Vand Chhakna encourages Sikhs to live by a principle of generosity, even self-sacrifice. Guru Amar Das, the third Guru, introduced to the Sikh community the idea of **daswandh**, or giving a tenth of surplus wealth to the service of the community. Any donations made through daswandh are used for such things as building schools or hospitals, or for famine or other disaster relief. It is a matter for the individual's conscience to determine the level of their giving, using the daswandh principle as a guide.

> **Daswandh** – a tithe: giving a tenth of your surplus wealth to help others in the community.

Activities

Key Elements

1 Explain in your own words the sentence 'Within the Sikh dharam there is no division between the sacred and the secular'.

2 Make notes on the three dimensions (Nam Japna, Kirat Karna and Vand Chhakna) which underpin Sikh life.

3 Guru Amar Das introduced the idea of daswandh. What is it?

Think About It

4 a) Discuss what you understand by the words 'sacred' and 'secular' with others in your group.
   b) What do you think about it?
   c) Are there sacred and secular elements to life?

5 Think about how the three dimensions of Nam Japna, Kirat Karna and Vand Chhakna might affect the way in which a Sikh lives.

6 Why would some Sikhs not work in a tobacconist shop or in a brewery, whilst other Sikhs sell cigarettes and alcohol in their shops?

7 a) Discuss what you think would be suitable and unsuitable occupations for a Sikh to engage in.
   b) Make a list of these in two columns.

8 How important do you think it is for a person's religion to set guidelines by which they should live (e.g. daswandh)?

Food

Friend, avoid that food which harms the body or provokes evil thoughts.

Adi Granth 16

Although the Gurus did not forbid the eating of meat (except *halal* – meat that had been killed and prepared in the special way required by Muslims), many Sikhs are vegetarians or eat meat only irregularly. In India eating meat was traditionally thought to produce such things as a bad temper, high blood pressure and even some forms of cancer. It follows then that in putting the words of Guru Nanak above into practice many Sikhs choose to avoid meat.

Vegetarian food is served in the langar. Also - how can you tell the man in the photograph is a Sikh? (Clue: what is he wearing?)

Vegetarian food is always served in the langar in order not to embarrass or offend anyone. People who eat meat are not compromised eating vegetarian food in the way that vegetarians would be if meat were served. The sharing of the food in the langar is an expression of the Sikh belief in hospitality and equality. Cleanliness is important in the storing, processing and eating of food.

In the Punjab, where the majority of Sikhs still live, a variety of pulses and vegetables, bread (chappatis), dairy products, milk and ghee (clarified butter) form the staple diet. Meat may be eaten very occasionally, usually at festival times. In Britain, many Sikhs continue to eat similar things as in the Punjab and to cook it in similar ways. However, pizzas, chips, crisps and other forms of fast food are popular, particularly with young people.

You don't have to have traditional Punjabi food is you are a Sikh. There is no rule against enjoying pizza and chips!

Drugs

Any form of non-medicinal drug is forbidden to Sikhs. In the vows made on becoming initiated into the Khalsa (see page 23) a promise is made not to use intoxicants and drugs. Guru Nanak taught that they clouded the mind and took people away from their first duty - to meditate on the name of God. They are unneccesary and can lead to addiction. He said:

Why should one who deals in the nectar of God's name develop a love for mere wine?

Adi Granth 360

This means that the vast majority of Sikhs do not drink alcohol or smoke tobacco. If they do however, they are not allowed to be on the managment committee of a gurdwara and some might find themselves excluded from the sangat (the congregation) until they had stopped.

Marriage, Sex and Contraception

Marriage is regarded very highly within the Sikh tradition. Sikhs believe that it is within marriage that the sexual act should be enjoyed and therefore sex before marriage (pre-marital sex) or sex outside of marriage (adultery) is frowned upon.

There are no religious reasons why a married couple should not use contraception but many, particularly in the Punjab, are expected by their parents, and indeed the wider community, to have children early on in their married life. Abortion is not to be encouraged but it is allowed in certain circumstances. In 1969 the Indian Parliament reviewed its position and made abortion legal in cases of pregnancy resulting from rape or from the failure of a contraceptive device used by a married couple. The Takhts (the five centres of spiritual authority which make religious decisions affecting the whole Sikh community) have not objected to this law.

Marriage is regarded in the Sikh faith as a life-long commitment. However, divorce is allowed, for example in circumstances of cruelty or desertion.

Pacifism

Although peaceful and peace-loving, the Sikh faith does not encourage pacifism. Sikhs are to be prepared, if all else fails, to fight for what is right and to protect those weaker than themselves.

Belief in the soldier/saint is an important concept within the Sikh faith tradition. A number of the Gurus themselves were involved in armed conflict to protect not only fellow Sikhs but others who were being persecuted for their faith. The kirpan is not an offensive weapon but a symbol of being prepared to 'stand up and be counted' for the faith and for the needs of others.

Kirpan – from the Punjabi words 'kirpa', meaning act of kindness, and 'aan', meaning honour or respect.

This Sikh is patrolling in the grounds of the Golden Temple in Amritsar.

Remember: the Sikh faith does not encourage a detachment from the world or from the needs of others. All Sikhs should be involved with the world, and try to promote generosity and justice. Carrying a kirpan is a sign of this.

The Environment

Sikhs are encouraged to respect and enjoy the natural world. The spirit of God is present in nature and the glory of God is seen in it.

> *In nature we see God, and in nature we hear God speak. Nature inspires devotion, and in nature is the essence of joy and peace... Air, water, fire, earth, dust are all parts of nature. The omnipotent creator commands, observes and pervades nature.*
> *Adi Granth 464*

However wonderful and inspiring nature is, Sikhs are reminded that the world is impermanent. Just as God created it, so too God can destroy it. It came into existence by the will of God and it will disappear when God wills it. That said, Sikhs believe that God looks after and sustains the creation.

The natural environment is a gift from God and as such Sikhs are encouraged to care for it. Their skill as farmers and horticulturists is well known in India. The Punjab, a small region in relation to the size of India, is very fertile. This is due partly to the climate and the five rivers which make up the region, but also to the way in which it is farmed and looked after.

Activities
Key Elements

1 a) What is a vegetarian?
   b) Why are many Sikhs vegetarian?
   c) Why is vegetarian food always served in the langar?

2 Why are Sikhs forbidden to use alcohol and other intoxicants?

3 What do Sikhs believe about the use of contraception?

Political and Social Action

We have already seen that Sikhs are not required to be pacifist. When all else fails, they may fight for what is right and to protect the weak.

From its early days, the Sikh community suffered persecurion. Two of the Gurus were killed for their faith. This has led some Sikhs to want an independent Sikh state, and even to try and achieve it by military means.

The Sikh community is divided between those who think it is right to take direct political action in this way and those who do not.

Maharaja Ranjit Singh

Around 150 years ago Sikhs in the Punjab were being persecuted. Some believed that the only way to end such persecution was to have a separate state. In 1799CE Maharaja Ranjit Singh, a young Sikh general, captured Lahore and established it as the capital of an independent Sikh state. He tried to put the Sikh belief in the equality of all into practice within the state, having Sikh, Muslim and Hindu members of government and of the armed forces. For around forty years he ruled this state using Sikh principles as his guide. Maharaja Ranjit Singh was also responsible for the restoration of the Harimandir (Golden Temple) in Amritsar. He died in 1839CE. The state then had ten years of instability - two leaders dying within six years and two wars. The British finally annexed the Punjab in 1849 and the independent Sikh homeland came to an end.

Maharaja Ranjit Singh

Khalistan

India gained its independence from the British Empire in 1947. Pakistan was also established as a Muslim country at this time. (It was later divided into Pakistan and Bangladesh.) The Punjab was divided between India and Pakistan which some Sikhs felt was very wrong. They called for a separate Sikh state, Khalistan, to be established. This did not happen. However, in 1966 it was agreed that the province of the Punjab should have Punjabi as its official language and that in the Punjabi Suba (provincial assembly) there would be a permanent Sikh majority in terms of its representatives. But even today there are still those amongst the Sikh community who want to go further and have a completely separate and independent homeland for the Sikhs. A few, despairing at making any progress by peaceful, political means have resorted to violence.

Sant Jarnail Singh Bhindranwhale

A focus for many wanting Khalistan to be established was Sant Jarnail Singh Bhindranwhale who led a group wanting independence for the Punjab during the 1970s. During this time and into the 1980s, the political situation in the Punjab was not good and indiscriminate attacks took place on a fairly regular basis. Sant Jarnail Singh Bhindranwhale was accused of organising violent opposition to the government, including being involved in attacks on the leader of a heretic Sikh group and on the editor of a Hindu newspaper. He was arrested but released very quickly. He went with some of his followers into the **Harimandir** for safety, reinforcing its defences and drawing on the stock of weapons in the Akal Takht. The Indian government decided to remove them from the Harimandir and the army, led by a Sikh officer, attacked on 1 June 1984. Sant Jarnail Singh Bhindranwhale and his followers resisted but after a hard fought fight, lasting five days and in which over a thousand people died, they were defeated.

This picture, displayed in a gurdwara in Britain, is an artist's impression of the damage to the Akal Takht in 1984.

Amongst the dead was Sant Jarnail Singh Bhindranwhale. Some Sikhs, particularly the young, look to him as an example of courage and devotion, a defender of the faith and its holy places. Some regard him as a martyr. His death has caused many to re-examine their own commitment to the Sikh way of life.

Continuing Unrest

Later in 1984, the then Prime Minister of India, Mrs Indira Gandhi was killed by two of her bodyguards. These men were Sikhs and the assassination resulted in violence between the Sikh and Hundu communities in which many innocent people were hurt. It has been estimated that during the 1980s over 25,000 have died in the conflict. That conflict has continued into the 1990s. In August 1995 Beant Singh, the Chief Minister of the state of Punjab was also assassinated as part of the ongoing political unrest.

There are other Sikhs who do not want a separate Sikh state and who are members of the Indian government, army officers and civil servants. There are others, who though they oppose the government's position on the Punjab, are against the use of force by a minority of Sikh activists.

Activities

Key Elements

1 Who was Maharaja Ranjit Singh?

2 When did India gain its independence from the British Empire?

3 What did some Sikhs call for at that time?

4 Who was Sant Jarnail Singh Bhindranwhale?

5 What happened in June 1984?

Think About It

6 (i) Copy out the statements below and identify them as being either true or false. For example, if you think that statement (a) is true, copy it out and in a different coloured pen write 'T' or 'true' at the end of the sentence.

   a) The majority of Sikhs are vegetarian.

   b) Some Sikhs do eat meat, particularly at festival times.

   c) Sometimes, meat is served in the langar.

   d) There is no restriction on whether or not a Sikh drinks alcohol or smokes tobacco.

   e) Sex before, or outside of, marriage is against what Sikhs believe.

   f) Abortion is frowned on as a means of contraception.

   g) Divorce is allowed within the Sikh faith under certain circumstances.

   h) The majority of Sikhs are pacifists.

   i) A Sikh would say that the natural world is for humankind's benefit and therefore we can do as we please with it.

   j) Sikhs do not believe that God created the world or that God cares for it now.

(ii) Discuss these statements and whether they are true or false with others in your group.

(iii) Re-write any statements you identified as false in a way which would make them true. Share what you have written with others in your group.

7 Should there be an independent Sikh state?

8 Is violence ever justified in bringing about social and political change?

9 Some people are looked up to as examples to follow. What sort of people do you think they are? Who do you look up to? What sort of example do you set to others?

Assignments

1 a) Draw up and conduct a survey to sample what people think about God. Try to get a cross-section of people to take part in it.

   b) Share your results with others.

   c) What conclusions, if any, can you make from the results of the survey?

2 Interview a Sikh about his or her understanding of God and of the purpose of human life.

3 a) Choose one of the issues raised in this section - vegetarianism; the use of alcohol and tobacco; marriage; divorce; sex and contraception - and research further into Sikh attitudes to it.

   b) Find out what other faiths say about the issue you have chosen.

   c) Present a summary of your findings to the rest of the class.

6

Worship

- The Gurdwara
- Diwan

- Private Devotions

God, the only God, pervades everywhere; as there is none other like him, to whom else can we offer worship?
Adi Granth 1345 - the words of Guru Nanak

...meditate on your Lord as long as you have breath.
Adi Granth 724 - the words of Guru Arjan

These words, paraphrased from the Guru Granth Sahib, explain the essence of all worship within Sikhism. Worship is to be centred on, and offered to, Akal Purakh, the Eternal, Timeless One, the one who alone is worthy of all praise and worship, and through the knowledge of whom individuals can find peace and fulfilment. Sikhs are required in their worship to call to mind the name of God and through this be drawn closer into the presence of God. **Nam Simran** in a literal translation from Punjabi into English means 'remembering the name of God' which is the essence of all Sikh worship.

Another important element of Sikh worship is **sewa**, literally translated to mean 'selfless service'; the outworking of the worship of the God who is everywhere and in everyone. As an important aspect of their worship Sikhs should offer selfless service to the sangat (the congregation of Sikhs), for the upkeep of the gurdwara and towards humanity in general.

Worship within Sikhism has both public and private aspects to it. Communal worship in the gurdwara is important in helping an individual to focus on God; private meditation and prayer are also important.

Communal worship focuses on the physical presence of the Guru Granth Sahib, regarded as the Guru living among the people as they worship. The Guru Granth Sahib is made up almost entirely of shabads (hymns) set in ragas (musical groupings) which are meant to be sung and which form the framework for the worship offered. Through music the worshippers receive the revelation (**bani**) of God as expressed in the words of the Holy Granth.

The devotional singing of the shabads to musical accompaniment is known as **kirtan**. Kirtan is considered to be a means of salvation as it helps the worshippers to become less self-centred and more God-centred.

This is a purpose built Gurdwara in Slough. Notice the Nishan Sahib on its flagpole.

Sikh worship can take place anywhere so long as it is in the presence of the Guru Granth Sahib. A place set aside for Sikh worship is called a gurdwara, which literally means 'the door (**dwara**) or house of the Guru'.

Gurdwaras, like places of worship within other faith traditions, are different in size and shape. Some are large buildings with elaborate decorations both inside and out; others are much smaller and humbler in character. In England some gurdwaras have been especially built, while others have been converted from a terraced house, or a church no longer required by a local Christian faith community.

Although there are differences between gurdwaras there are always some common features.

The Nishan Sahib, the Gurus' symbol, flies outside every gurdwara to indicate a Sikh place of worship and langar (see page 25). The Nishan Sahib is mounted on a pole covered in the same saffron coloured cloth. The Nishan Sahib and the cloth covering the flagpole are renewed annually as part of the Baisakhi celebrations. The Khanda may also be seen inside the gurdwara.

Many other Gurdwaras, like this one in Peterborough, are in converted houses.

Inside the prayer hall.

Inside the Gurdwara

The focal point of the gurdwara's prayer hall (**Darbar Sahib**) is the Guru Granth Sahib, which must be in a prominent position so that it can be clearly seen from every part of the room. There is no set direction in which the prayer hall should face, as the Guru Granth Sahib provides the focal point for worship. A space is left behind the Guru Granth Sahib to allow the **granthi** (reader) to move freely (see also page 82 on the marriage ceremony).

There is no seating inside the prayer hall. The worshippers sit on the floor facing the Scriptures. This emphasises the unique place which the Guru Granth Sahib holds, as it alone is raised. It also symbolises the attitude of humility which worshippers should have, and their equality as rich and poor, young and old, male and female, in the presence of the Holy Granth.

The langar (kitchen) is also a common feature of a gurdwara. It represents service towards others, an important aspect of worship. It is considered a privilege to help prepare and serve the food which is provided for all, free of charge.

The Function of a Gurdwara

Each gurdwara has a management committee which is elected by the community and responsible to it. Elections may take place every year or in some cases every two years, usually at Baisakhi time. Members of the management committee are not paid, they give of their time and efforts freely. It is considered an honour to be elected to the management committee of the gurdwara.

Besides the daily services in the gurdwara there are other services, festivals and ceremonies to accommodate: the **Sangrand** service on the first day of every solar month, the annual festivals of Baisakhi and Divali, as well as naming, wedding, initiation and funeral ceremonies.

In Britain weddings and funerals are more closely associated with the gurdwara building than they would be in the Punjab where these ceremonies would probably take place out of doors. Weddings often take place in Britain during the Sunday service. A funeral service is held in the prayer hall of the gurdwara before going to the crematorium; the coffin is left in the entrance hall or another appropriate place.

The interior of a typical gurdwara.

- Copy and label this outline of a gurdwara, using the information given in this chapter.
- Make notes on the features you have labelled.

At other times families or individuals may ask for an **Akhand Path**, the continuous reading of the Guru Granth Sahib, to mark some special event - a forthcoming marriage or the death of a member of the family. This reading takes about 48 hours. Often the family members will liaise with the granthi and the committee over providing a series of people to take part in the reading. They would try to be there for as much of the reading as possible. Sometimes the Akhand Path will take place in a home which has been specially prepared (cleaned etc.) to receive the Guru Granth Sahib.

The Gurdwara as a Community Centre

Gurdwaras are, and always have been, not only places of worship but also centres where the Sikh community can gather together. This is consistent with the Sikh view of worship, it is about, and affects, the whole of life. In India many gurdwaras provide accommodation for travellers, and following the example set to them by Guru Har Rai, some have dispensaries or clinics attached to them.

In Britain many gurdwaras also act as social centres for the local Sikh community. Some have begun to hold classes in Punjabi to help children to learn, understand and read the language of the Guru Granth Sahib. (It also helps retain links with their parents', or in some cases their grandparents', first language.)

Question
- Why do you think the gurdwara is more than just a place of worship?

Music classes, youth clubs and women's groups are other activities which may be held in the gurdwara. Rooms are often used on a less formal basis for friends to socialise. Also, in Britain, the gurdwara is used for weddings and funerals in a way not common in India, where many more activities take place outside.

Learning Punjabi at the gurdwara.

Location

In India some gurdwaras are linked with an event in the life of one of the Gurus. For example, there is a gurdwara in Goindwal, associated with Guru Amar Das, where he established his headquarters. He summoned Sikhs to meet there three times a year during the great Hindu festivals, so encouraging their Sikh identity.

Gurdwaras are found in many major, and smaller, towns and cities of Britain, wherever Sikhs are represented within the community.

Harimandir

The Harimandir is set in an artificial lake, and reached by a causeway.

The Harimandir, built on the instigation of Guru Arjan in Amritsar, was an important milestone in the development of worship within Sikhism. It was here that Guru Arjan installed the Adi Granth. It became a focus for Sikh worship and identity and it remains so today. The pattern for worship which developed in the Harimandir has provided the inspiration for worship in gurdwaras worldwide.

The Harimandir features widely in Sikh art, as on this wall hanging.

In a ceremony which is performed in every Gurdwara, the Guru Granth Sahib is carried out of the Harimandir in a procession each evening. Pilgrims crowd around it as it is carried over the causeway.

Diwan

A Granthi reads from the Guru Granth Sahib in an act of worship. Notice the Sikhs at the front of the congregation are wearing traditional dress. They have gathered to celebrate the opening of a new gurdwara.

Congregational worship within Sikhism is based on and around the Guru Granth Sahib. In addition to this some passages from the Dasam Granth may be read. Explanation of these and addresses on matters affecting the community - moral, social and political - also forms part of the time of worship together. Music and singing are important expressions of worship for Sikhs. The sharing of karah parshad at the end of the service and eating in the langar are also important elements, pointing as they do to the equality and unity which is expressed through the Holy Granth. Worship is conducted in Punjabi.

Gurdwaras do not have fixed opening times, nor fixed times for worship to begin and end. Services carry on over a long period of time, but individuals are free to come and go as they please - some stay only a short time, others for longer periods. There is no special day for worship as there is in other faith traditions (e.g. Friday for Muslims). In Britain, the largest daytime congregations for Sikh worship tend to be on a Sunday, as this is the day when most people do not go to work. During the rest of the week services often take place in the evening.

The granthi will begin reading from the Guru Granth Sahib at dawn. It is brought from its resting place and installed in the prayer hall.

The granthi then opens it at random and reads the first passage on the left hand page. This first lesson of the day is called the Vak laina and is regarded as the Guru's message for the day. This will be brought to the attention of all who visit the gurdwara that day through a notice on the notice board, informing everyone of the passage chosen. The granthi continues to read from the Guru Granth Sahib until it is judged there are enough people present for kirtan to begin. Some people may call in to the gurdwara to worship on their way to work. Retired people may attend in the early morning also.

The Guru Granth Sahib in Worship

The Guru Granth Sahib is the focal point of Sikh worship. Its importance is symbolised in many ways, by how it is treated and the respect which it is shown.

At the beginning of the day, when it is brought from its resting place, it is carried in procession on the head of a respected member of the community. Members of the congregation bow as it enters. This process is repeated in reverse when it is returned to its resting place in the evening.

In the prayer hall it has pride of place. It is placed on a **takht** (a raised platform). On the platform is a **palki**, an arched structure which covers the **manji** (large stool) where the Guru Granth Sahib is placed. **Romallas** (fine clothes), which have usually been donated by members of the congregation, cover the manji. When the Holy Granth is not being read the romallas cover it.

The granthi (reader) sits behind the Guru Granth Sahib. To the side, space is left for the ragis (musicians) and their instruments - the most common being the **baja**, a sort of harmonium and the **jorri** or **tabla**, a kind of drum. In front of it people place their offerings (for example money, food for the langar, a romalla, flowers).

The granthi will from time to time wave a chauri, a type of fan, over the Holy Granth. The chauri can be made from yak hair or a synthetic material. Its is as a sign of respect for, and submission to, the sovereignty of the Holy Granth.

Before entering the prayer hall shoes will have been removed, heads covered and, probably, hands washed - some will have taken a bath before coming to the gurdwara. Then the

A chauri.

worshippers will make their way to the front and bow low on their knees before the Guru Granth Sahib, the majority touching the ground with their forehead, as a sign of respect. After placing their offering in front of the Guru Granth Sahib they will move away, not turning their backs on it. Worshippers sit on the floor facing the front; men sit on one side and women on the other. It is considered to be disrespectful to point the soles of the feet towards the Holy Granth and so the worshippers will sit cross legged or with their feet pointing away from it.

The Guru Granth Sahib is always the focal point of worship.

Worshippers may enter or leave the prayer hall at any time. On leaving they should stand, bow towards the Guru Granth Sahib with their hands together as a sign of submission to the will of Raheguru (God), as expressed through the words of the Scriptures, before departing. Again they should be careful not to turn their back towards the Holy Granth.

Sikh worshippers place offerings before the Guru Granth Sahib. Notice that, looking across the Gurdwara, you see only the women and children. This is because the men sit on one side and the women on the other. Some people make offerings of money, others offer other things. Notice the bottles of milk - this is for use in the langar.

The Granthi

There is no priesthood in Sikhism but the Guru Granth Sahib has to be cared for properly, worship and other ceremonies conducted, gurdwara activities planned and overseen. In some gurdwaras a full time granthi is appointed and supported to do this, in others it is done by a person in a voluntary and part-time capacity. In small villages in the Punjab, for example, the granthi is more likely to be part-time and unpaid and combine his duties with other employment. Most of the larger gurdwaras in India will have full-time staff. In Britain many, though not all, gurdwaras also have full-time staff.

Even if a gurdwara does have a full-time granthi, others will also lead worship. Any member of the congregation, male or female, who is able to can lead worship by reading from the Guru Granth Sahib and leading kirtan (devotional singing).

In Britain the granthi also has prime responsibility for the pastoral care of the community, although each member should play their part in comforting the bereaved and visiting the sick.

Kirtan

Kirtan is the name given to the devotional singing of shabads which forms such an important part of Sikh worship. It is believed that kirtan helps the worshippers to become less self-centred and more reliant upon God. It is a way of centring one's thoughts, emotions, will and spirit on God which is the goal of Sikh

Musicians playing in the gurdwara.

life and worship. At the beginning of kirtan a passage from Guru Nanak is read and then other shabads are sung. The choice of these may depend on a particular event being celebrated (for example, the anniversary of Guru Arjan's birthday) or it may be the choice of those leading worship that day. Often there is some explanation of what is to be sung.

Kirtan is interspersed with talks, sermons and lectures. These may be given by those responsible for leading worship that day or there may be a visitor from India or from another gurdwara who has been asked to speak. The aim of these is to help the worshipper understand the words they are hearing from the Guru Granth Sahib and to put them into practice in their daily lives both as individuals and as a community. They will often contain stories from the lives of the Gurus and others as examples to look to as well as encouraging the people to live good, moral lives.

The Ardas

The conclusion of the service is known as the Ardas. Here is an eye-witness account of Ardas from a non-Sikh visitor to a gurdwara in London. Afterwards a Sikh friend explained what happened.

'In drawing the service to its conclusion the people sang what I later found to be called the Anand and then we all stood. One man from the congregation moved to stand in front of the Guru Granth Sahib and recited what my friend said was the Japji.
Many of the congregation stood with their palms together, either straight out in front of them, or with fingers just touching their chins. Some had their heads bowed. Some joined in the chanting, others didn't.
As the congregation continued their prayers another person came out from the congregation, uncovered

a metal bowl which was to the front and side of the Guru Granth Sahib and stirred the contents using a metal knife. After the prayers ended we all sat again and three people brought around the contents of the bowl and gave a small portion of it (into the right hand) to all those present. This is karah parshad which is shared at the close of all Sikh services. I found it to be very sweet. The final prayers took about fifteen minutes altogether. Someone then stood at the front and gave out some notices before we went into the dining area to have a vegetarian meal together which had been prepared on the premises.'

Question

- What is the Sikh name for the 'metal knife' refered to in the account of Ardas from a non-Sikh visitor?

The Ardas prayer brings services to a close. The prayer encourages Sikhs to remember their Gurus, the teachings of the Guru Granth Sahib and asks God's blessing on the Sikh community and the whole of humanity.

The Ardas prayer is about four hundred words long. Here is a translation of some selected extracts from it:

Let the whole Khalsa bring to mind the Name of the Wonderful Lord ... May the kingdom of justice come. May Sikhs be united in love. May the hearts of Sikhs be humble but their wisdom exalted - their wisdom in the keeping of the Lord, O Khalsa, say 'Waheguru' ... Save us from lust, wrath, greed, undue attachment and pride; and keep us always attached to Your feet ... We offer this prayer in Your presence. Raheguru, forgive us our sins. Help us to keep ourselves pure ... And may all prosper by Your grace.

At the end of the day, the Guru Granth Sahib is carried out of the gurdwara and put in its resting place for the night, covered with beautiful cloths. Every gurdwara has a small place set aside as the Guru Granth Sahib's 'bedroom'.

Private Devotions

He who calls himself a Sikh of the great Sat Guru should rise early in the morning and meditate on God's name ... by repeating God's name according to the Guru's instructions, all evil deeds and mistakes will be washed away. At sunrise he should sing the bani and all through the busy day, he should discipline his mind to live in God's presence. The Guru's disciple who contemplates God with every breath and with every bite of food, become pleasing to the Guru's mind.

(Adi Granth 305: the words of Guru Ram Das)

The ideal for personal prayer and devotion as set out in the Guru Granth Sahib is demanding.

A dedication and discipline is expected which will bring fulfilment and happiness as a worshipper becomes less self-centred and more centred on God, the source of all true happiness. The Guru Granth Sahib makes this point very forcibly, 'Being self centred we die: becoming God centred we live' (Adi Granth:1238).

Bathing before saying prayers or going to the gurdwara is not so much the idea of cleansing and forgiveness, as in some other religious traditions, but emphasises the relationship which exists between God and the worshipper. God surrounds and is within.

At dawn the worshipper should repeat the **Japji** of Guru Nanak and the **Jap** and **Swayyas** from Guru Gobind Singh to help them to meditate on the name of God. Some Sikhs would also use a **mala** to help them in their meditation. A mala is a prayer rope made up of 108 knots which are passed through the fingers as the believer repeats 'Raheguru' (Wonderful Lord). Some may then go to the gurdwara to join in the early morning worship there before the work of the day begins.

In the evening there are two more set hymns to repeat, one at dusk (**Rahiras**) and one before going to bed for the night (**Sohilla**). The mala may again be used as an aid to meditation.

Many Sikhs will not have a personal copy of the Guru Granth Sahib but use a gutka instead (see page 40 for more detail regarding this point).

Some Sikhs use a mala in their private devotions.

Activities

Key Elements

1 What does the word gurdwara mean?

2 What is the focal point of Sikh worship?

3 What is a granthi?

4 a) What do worshippers do before entering the prayer hall?
b) What do they do when they go into the prayer hall?

5 What do the words 'Nam Simran' and 'sewa' mean?

6 What is the devotional singing of the shabads known as?

7 Where can Sikh communal worship take place?

8 What is an Akhand Path?

9 What is a mala?

Think About It

10 Some Sikhs use a mala to help them in the private devotions and prayer. How do you think it might help them?

11 Discuss in groups

a) The word 'worship'. You may like to brainstorm first in order to give you a framework for your discussion. How does your discussion about worship relate to anything you have discovered about Sikh worship after reading this chapter?

b) Why is the presence of the Guru Granth Sahib such an important part of Sikh worship?

c) Read the selected extract from the Ardas prayer which concludes Sikh community worship. (i) What do you think a Sikh would understand by it? (ii) How might it affect the way in which a Sikh might live their life (their beliefs, relationships with other Sikhs, relationships with those who are not Sikh)?

Assignment

1 Choose at least one section from question 11 above and write a paragraph about it following your discussions.

7

Festivals and Pilgrimage

- Gurpurbs
- Melas

- Pilgrimage
- Some Special Places

Two types of festival are celebrated by Sikhs - **gurpurbs** and **melas**.

Gurpurbs

A gurpurb is essentially a holy day in honour of a Guru. The word is derived from two Punjabi words - guru (teacher) and purb (holiday). Gurpurbs are celebrations connected with the birth or death of one of the ten Gurus. The four most commonly celebrated gurpurbs by British Sikhs are the birthdays of Guru Nanak and Gobind Singh and the martyrdoms of Guru Arjan and Tegh Bahadur. Other anniversaries, like that of the installation of the Adi Granth in 1604CE are also gurpurbs.

Congregational worship takes place to celebrate gurpurbs, as does an Akhand Path, the continuous reading of the Guru Granth Sahib which is timed to reach its conclusion as a major part of the festivities. There may also be a street procession of the Guru Granth Sahib, particularly on the gurpurb which celebrates the birth of Guru Nanak, and also to mark the birthday of Guru Gobind Singh. In Britain some gurdwaras put up banners, to tell all those around of the special gurpurb being celebrated. Sometimes a firework display might also be arranged.

Some Important Gurpurbs
October/November - the birthday of Guru Nanak
December - the birthday of Guru Gobind Singh
May/June - the martyrdom of Guru Arjan
November/December - the martyrdom of Guru Tegh Bahadur

Melas

A mela is a fair. Melas are times of celebrations which coincide with important Hindu festivals.

Baisakhi, Divali and Hola Mohalla are melas. Originally Hindu festivals, they are now celebrated by Sikhs. Guru Amar Das began the tradition of his followers gathering together at Baisakhi and Divali, and Guru Gobind Singh called them together at Hola Mohalla. In this way not only did they have opportunities to listen to their Guru they were also distinguished, as Sikhs, from their Hindu neighbours.

Baisakhi

During the time of the tenth Guru, Sikhs were being persecuted and discriminated against because of their faith. It was against this background that the Khalsa was formed (for more details about the founding of the Khalsa at Baisakhi 1699 CE see Chapter 3).

At Baisakhi time Sikhs also remember a massacre which happened in Amritsar in 1919 when a British General (Dyer) ordered troops to fire on the assembled Sikh crowd. It is also the first day of the Sikh new year and it is usually the day on which gurdwara committees are elected.

An important part of the Baisakhi celebrations is to renew the Nishan Sahib which has been flying outside the gurdwara over the course of the previous year. The cloth which has been wrapped around the flag pole is also renewed at this time. The flag pole is taken down and washed in yoghurt (a symbol of purity and cleanliness) before being wrapped in clean cloths and a new flag attached to it. The cloths and the flag are donated by members of the congregation.

In the Punjab many Sikhs would try to visit Amritsar for Baisakhi (which coincides with a huge animal fair held outside the city). A political rally is held in the afternoon at Jallianwala Bagh (the site of the 1919 massacre). Bhangra dancing and processions form part of the celebrations.

In this country street processions are sometimes arranged for Baisakhi by a local gurdwara. Cards may be sent to family and friends to wish them a happy Baisakhi time and many Sikhs would visit the gurdwara to share in the worship and celebrations.

Getting the flagpole down at Baisakhi.

Cleaning the flagpole with yoghurt at Baisakhi.

Assignment
Find out more about Bhangra dancing.

Bhangra dancing in the Punjab (above) and also among Sikh students in the West.

Divali

Divali was, and remains, a festival celebrated by Hindus, remembering the return of Prince Rama from fourteen years in exile. Why then does the Sikh community celebrate this festival?

The connection is with the sixth Guru, Guru Hargobind, who was imprisoned by the Mughal authorities at a time when Sikhs were being persecuted for their faith. He was in prison in the town of Gwalior along with more than fifty Hindu princes (rajas). Jehingir, the Emperor, investigated the charges brought against the Guru and found them to be false. He ordered that Guru Hargobind be released immediately but the Guru refused to be released unless his fellow captives were also set free. Jehingir decreed that as many as could hold onto the Guru's clothes as he walked to freedom through the narrow passage which led out of the prison would also be released. The Guru asked for a cloak to be brought to him. This cloak had long tassels on it and each raja was able to hold onto it and thus walk to freedom with Guru Hargobind. This all happened at Divali time and since then Sikhs have made the celebration their own as they remember the safe return of their Guru.

Guru Hargobind leading the prisoners out of prison.

Bonfires and fireworks make the festival an exciting time. Some try to journey to Amritsar where the Harimandir is very richly illuminated by clay lamps and lights but those who can't might place clay lamps (divas) on the doorsteps of gurdwaras, on the gateposts or garden walls, and in the windows of their homes.

Divali lights.

Hola Mohalla

Hola Mohalla was instituted by Guru Gobind Singh in the year following the formation of the Khalsa at Baisakhi 1699 CE.

Guru Gobind Singh called his followers together the following spring at Anandpur in northern India at the time of the Hindu festival of Holi, held in honour of the god Krishna. He did so as a means of developing the Sikh identity of his followers. He asked them to bring their weapons in order that they should take part in training manoeuvres. Since that time Sikhs have celebrated Hola Mohalla by means of archery contests, wrestling matches and other such activities. Many gurdwaras would organise sporting activities and competitions as part of these festival celebrations.

When Melas are celebrated:
April – Baisakhi
October/November – Divali
February/March – Hola Mohalla

Some of the many sports and competitions that take place at Hola Mohalla. In gurdwaras in Britain, rounders, races and football matches are popular.

Pilgrimage

A feature of almost all religions is pilgrimage to holy places, usually associated with a founder or spiritual leader or with some historical, mythological or spiritual event in their history. In some religions pilgrimage is a very important aspect of the life and devotion of the people. For example, in the Hindu faith tradition there are countless places of pilgrimage, some well known to many Hindus but others more local or regional. Within the Muslim faith tradition pilgrimage to Makkah is an obligation on all those who are able to make the journey. There are important places which are connected with the origin and development of the faith which many Sikhs will try to visit but pilgrimage is not an obligation.

> *True pilgrimage consists of the contemplation of the name of God and the cultivation of inner knowledge.*
>
> Adi Granth 687

> *There is no place of pilgrimage equal to the Guru's. The Guru alone is the pool of contentment. The Guru is the river from which pure water is obtained, by which the dirt of evil understanding is washed away.*
>
> Adi Granth 1,328

> *If someone goes to bathe at a place of pilgrimage with the mind of a crook and the body of a thief then his outside will have been washed but his inside will be dirty twice over ... The saints are good even without such washing. The thief remains a thief even if they bathe at a place of pilgrimage.*
>
> Adi Granth 789

Activity

- Look at the photographs of pilgrims on this page and page 71. Write down what you imagine they would be thinking and feeling as they visit this place.

Amritsar is an important place of pilgrimage for Sikhs. Pilgrims take part in celebrations, but may also spend time in private prayer, inspired by being in such a holy place.

At the time of the Gurus their followers gathered wherever the Guru happened to be, or where he told them he would be for a particular period. They gathered together to hear his teaching and to learn more about putting it into practice in their daily lives. However, many of them were used to places of pilgrimage, particularly those associated with water and cleansing, since many of the Gurus' early followers were from Hindu backgrounds. Following the teachings of their Gurus, Sikhs reject the idea of ceremonial bathing and pilgrimage bringing about cleansing or reward.

Yet there are places which have become important symbols of the faith for many Sikhs and places to which some Sikhs will go in a spirit of devotion to God. Guru Amar Das had a deep well constructed at Goindwal. After it was completed the tradition of taking a bath in it, and reciting the Japji on each of its 84 steps began. It was said that a person who had done this would obtain freedom from the continuing cycle of births and deaths. The emphasis, however, is not on the ritual but on the recitation of the divine name - meditation.

Washing is an important feature of many religions. Water cleans and purifies. Although Sikhs reject the idea of ceremonial bathing for its own sake, many who visit Amritsar - like the man in this photograph - bathe in the water of the artificial lake that surrounds the 'Golden Temple', or Harimandir.

Fact Box

The Japji (or Jap Sahib), which pilgrims may recite as they go down the steps at Goindwal, is the meditation from Guru Gobind Sing's Dasam Granth (see p44).

Here is an extract from it, referring to pilgrimage:

Pilgrimage, austerity, mercy, almsgiving and charity,
Bring merit, be it as little as the mustard seed,
But those who hear, believe and cherish the word, An inner pilgrimage and cleansing is their's.

Activities

- Look carefully at the three paraphases of words from the Guru Granth Sahib and the words of the Japji which make reference to pilgrimage. From these words what do you understand Sikh attitudes towards pilgrimage to be?

- How important do you think pilgrimage to a special place is, or should be, as part of a person's religion? Discuss your thoughts about these things with others in your group.

Some Special Places

Amritsar

Amritsar literally means the 'Pool of Nectar' and is on land given by the Emperor Akbar to Guru Ram Das and his followers. It was first called **Chak Ramdas** or **Ramdaspur** because it was Guru Ram Das who started to build it. A small natural pool already existed but the Guru had it enlarged. His son, Guru Arjan, continued it and built the Harimandir which now stands in the middle of the pool.

The Harimandir is often referred to as the Golden Temple because it is covered in sheets of gilded copper and so looks golden. Also, much of the artwork on the doors and ceilings inside is gold. The Temple has two storeys. Inside there is a lot of black and white marble which contributes to making it a very beautiful building. Sikhs often refer to it as the **Darbar Sahib** which means 'the court of the Lord'. As a symbol of humility before God, the Temple was built so that those going inside have to step down in order to enter. There are doors on all four sides which symbolises the Sikh way of life being open to all.

Many Sikh homes and gurdwaras in this country will have a picture of the Harimandir.

Crowds of pilgrims make their way across the 'Pool of Nectar' to the Harimandir.

The Five Takhts

Name	Place	Connection
Akal Takht	Amritsar	Foundations laid by Guru Hargobind
Takht Harimandir	Patna	Birthplace of Guru Gobind Singh
Takht Keshgarh	Anandpur	Foundation of the Khalsa
Takht Damdama Sahib	Talwandi Sabo	Final version of Guru Granth Sahib
Takht Hazur	Nanded	Assassination of Guru Gobind Singh

At Amritsar, the **Akal Takht** faces the Harimandir. Its foundations were laid by Guru Hargobind. Its name means 'throne of the Timeless One'. (The Punjabi word 'takht' means 'throne'.)

There are five major Takhts which act as places of spiritual authority where the most important decisions affecting the whole Sikh community are taken. These decisions are made after discussions between the leaders of the five Takhts and the granthi at the Harimandir. Interpretation of the meaning of passages from the Holy Granth can also come from the Takhts. The Akal Takht at Amritsar is regarded by some as the most influential of the Takhts although others would disagree saying that all five have equal authority.

The other four Takhts are all connected in some way with Guru Gobind Singh. The **Takht Harimandir** in Patna is at the place where the Guru was born. The **Takht Keshgarh** is in Anandpur and is connected with the foundation of the Khalsa. The **Takht Damdama Sahib** at Talwandi Sabo is where the final version of the Guru Granth Sahib was produced. The **Takht Hazur** at Nanded is at the place where the Guru was assassinated.

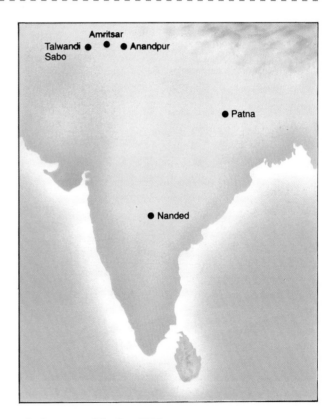

The location of the five Takhts.

The Akal Takht at Amritsar.

Fact Box

The Guru Granth Sahib is placed on a 'takht' in the prayer hall of the gurdwara. The takht is a symbol of the authority which it has in the life and worship of the Sikh community.

Activities

Key Elements

1 What are the two main types of Sikh festival?

2 Copy out the charts on pages 66 and 69, which give examples of each of the types of festival celebrated by Sikhs.

3 Choose one festival of each type and make notes about when, how and why it is celebrated.

4 What does the word Amritsar mean?

5 What was Amrtisar originally called? Who started its construction and who completed it?

6 What is the Harimandir?

7 What does the word 'takht' mean?

8 What is the purpose of the Five Takhts within the Sikh community?

Think About It

9 Festival celebrations are often very symbolic. What do you understand by the words 'symbol' and 'symbolic'?

10 Why are the Five Takhts important centres of authority within the Sikh community?

11 The Harimandir is thought of by many as a very beautiful building. Why do many people of different faith traditions build big and beautiful buildings like this?

12 'Pilgrimage of the heart is more important than to a place, but my visit to Goindwal deepened my faith in God and the Gurus.' What does this statement tell you about Sikh teaching about pilgrimage?

13 If possible, talk to Sikhs about how they have celebrated a festival. What happened? How did they feel before, during and after the celebrations?

Assignment

1 Imagine that you are a young Sikh who has just visited Amritsar for the first time. Write either a diary of your visit or a letter to one of your friends explaining what you saw, what you did and something about how you felt.

8

Ceremonies

- Birth
- The Amrit Sanskar
- Marriage
- Death

Special events in the life of individuals are important not only to that individual and their immediate family, but also sometimes to society as a whole. For example, in Britain, when teenagers reach the age of 18 they are officially recognised as adults. That recognition brings with it responsibilities, like being able to vote in parliamentary elections.

Although there is no formal ceremony, many families choose to hold a special party for the person who has become 18. They may also give him or her a special gift, to mark the transition to adulthood. Thus, a personal event can have a significance in the community as well as for the individual and his or her family.

Religious traditions often mark significant events in the life of individuals with some form of religious ceremony and observance.

The following events are usually focused upon:
- **Birth** - which often includes the ideas of thankfulness for a safe delivery and good wishes for the future;
- **Growing up** - which is often linked to ceremonies in which the person formally accepts the rights and responsibilities of belonging to the faith community;
- **Marriage** - in which their new relationship to each other, within their families and in society at large is recognised;
- **Death** - when the deceased life is remembered, their passing marked and beliefs about their continuing life expressed.

Together, these ceremonies are often referred to as being '**rites of passage**', since they are ceremonies which mark the transition (movement) from one stage of life to another.

Think About It

1 What have been the most important events in your life so far? Were they marked by some sort of religious ceremony? If so, what sort of ceremony was it? What happened?

2 Why do you think religious people choose to mark significant events, like birth, marriage and death, with special ceremonies?

Our journey (passage) through life.

In this chapter, we will focus on the rites of passage related to birth, marriage and death within the Sikh faith tradition before examining the Amrit Sanskar, the initiation ceremony for admission to the Khalsa.

Birth

'Is it a boy or a girl?' This is sometimes the first question to be asked on hearing of the birth of a child. Indeed parents are frequently asked, 'Do you want a girl or a boy?', even before the baby is born. These questions are often asked purely out of interest but they can reflect attitudes towards the different genders.

In many societies in the past the birth of a baby girl was not welcomed with as much rejoicing as that of a baby boy. Why might this be? Until recently in Britain, boys went out to work to help to support the family whereas girls were expected to work within the home until they married, rather than going out to earn money. This meant that they were often regarded as more of an economic liability than their brothers.

This continues to be the case in a country like India. With no universal social security system boys are expected to look after their parents in old age since the girls will have married and joined a new family. Often sons are also regarded as being more important for the continuation of the family line.

The Sikh faith's emphasis on the equality of all does not make it totally immune from these social and cultural pressures.

Within the Sikh faith the birth of a child is seen as strengthening the stability of marriage and ensuring the continuity of the family line. So the birth of a baby is cause for great rejoicing within the family and within the community.

About two weeks after the birth of the baby, the parents visit the gurdwara to present the child before the Guru Granth Sahib. Often relatives and friends will attend with them. The naming ceremony takes place towards the end of a service of worship or separately, although this is not usual. The parents will take a romalla and the ingredients or some money to pay for the karah parshad. They may also take along food to be shared in the langar after the service.

1. Water and sugar crystals are placed in a bowl and stirred with a 'Khanda'. This is done in front of the Guru Granth Sahib. The Mool Mantra and the first five verses of the Japji Sahib are read out.

2. A little of this mixture is dropped into the child's mouth from the end of a 'kirpan' and the rest is given to the mother to drink.

3. The Granthi opens the Guru Granth Sahib at random and reads a hymn. The child's name is chosen to begin with the first letter of this reading.

4. Everyone shares Karah Parshad

The naming ceremony.

Fact Box

Romalla: a piece of cloth, about a metre square, used to cover the Guru Granth Sahib.

Karah parshad: a sweet food distributed at the end of Sikh worship services.

Making a gift of a romalla and giving the ingredients or money for the making of karah parshad are traditional ways of showing thanksgiving.

The Ardas prayer is said and the granthi prays that the blessing of God will be upon the child. After these prayers the Holy Granth is opened at random, the choice being left to God. The top section of the left-hand page is read out and the first letter of the first word becomes the initial letter for the baby's name. The parents choose a name beginning with this letter and it is then announced to the congregation, adding Singh for a boy and Kaur for a girl.

For example, if the letter 'I' is the first letter on the left hand side of the page and the baby is a boy, then parents might choose the name Inderjit. If the letter were a 'K' and the baby a girl, then she might be called Kanwaljit. Some names are used for babies of either sex, for example, Jasbinder or Surinder. A boy would be called Surinder Singh and a girl Surinder Kaur. Some Sikhs choose not to use a family or surname while others do. Names such as Bhogal, Cheema, Chahal and Nijhar are Sikh family names.

Question

Surinder Singh Bhogal
Surinder Kaur Bhogal

- Which is the boy and which is the girl?
- How do you know?

The Anand Sahib is then sung, a prayer of thanksgiving for the name is offered and then the granthi gives amrit to the baby. Sugar crystals are dissolved in water and the opening words of the Japji are said over it. The tip of the khanda is then dipped into the prepared amrit and a little of the liquid dropped into the baby's mouth. Any that is left is given to the mother to drink.

The family might also arrange for an Akhand Path to take place to mark the celebrations. An Akhand Path is a continual reading of the Guru Granth Sahib.

Activities

Key Elements

1 Write a summary of the events of a Sikh naming ceremony.

2 How was your name chosen? Does it have a meaning?

Think About It

3 How important is a name?

4 Why do you think that it is important to Sikhs that names are chosen based on a letter from the Guru Granth Sahib?

Assignments

1 Conduct a survey of first names in your school. Which names are popular, which are more unusual? Find out the meanings of some of the names in your survey.

2 Find out how one other religious tradition celebrates the birth of a baby. Compare what happens with the Sikh naming ceremony.

The Amrit Sanskar

Details of the Amrit Sanskar, the Sikh initiation ceremony are given in chapter 3, which focuses on the Khalsa (see pages 26–27). Here it is mentioned within the context of being a ceremony which marks an important landmark in life and raises the question, 'What is a Sikh?'

The Amrit Sanskar is about being fully committed to the Sikh faith. By going through the ceremony the person is taking upon themselves full membership of the Khalsa with all that that entails (wearing the Panj Kakke, etc.) Not all Sikhs go through this ceremony to become initiated into the Khalsa. Those who do not are called **sahaj-dhari**, which means 'seekers after God', they may keep some of the Khalsa rules but have not as yet fully committed themselves to the Sikh faith by taking part in the Amrit Sanskar ceremony. Those who have taken part in the ceremony are known as **kesh-dhari** (kesh referring to their uncut hair).

A child born into a Sikh family and brought up in accordance with the Sikh faith is regarded as a Sikh. For those who were born Sikh the initiation ceremony symbolises a personal commitment to the religious and social requirements of the faith. Although the Sikh faith is not primarily a missionary religion those who convert to it go through the same ceremony; they add Singh or Kaur to their name and usually take a Punjabi first name to bring them closer to the roots of the faith.

It is important that the person understands the promises and obligations which come with the ceremony. Although there is no set age at which a person can decide to become part of the Khalsa it is usual to wait until mid-teens and some people are much older.

Unlike the naming and wedding ceremonies, the Amrit Sanskar does not usually take place during an ordinary worship service. It is customary for only those to be initiated, and those who have been initiated, to be present. Like other ceremonies it takes place in the presence of the Holy Granth.

Activity

- **Either**: a) Look up any notes you have taken on the foundation of the Khalsa, the Panj Kakke and the Amrit Sanskar from chapter 3 . Add any extra information you have gained from this page.

  Or: b) If you have no notes yet - make detailed notes on the foundation of the Khalsa, the Panj Kakke and the Amrit Sanskar, using the information in chapter 3 and this page as a basis.

Activities

Key Elements

1 What is the difference between a sahaj-dhari and a kesh-dhari Sikh?

2 What is the Amrit Sanskar ceremony about?

Think About It

3 Why do you think the Amrit Sanskar ceremony is such an important landmark in life for many Sikhs?

4 Look up the vows taken on becoming a member of the Khalsa on page 23. They are all important to the way in which Sikhs live their lives. They provide a sort of 'code of conduct'. What are the rules by which you live your life and make your decisions?

Activity

If possible talk to a Sikh who has not yet undergone the initiation ceremony and one who has.

Ask the sahaj-dhari Sikh why they have not as yet taken part in the Amrit Sanskar ceremony and if they intend to or not.

Ask the kesh-dhari Sikh why they underwent the Amrit Sanskar ceremony and what difference, if any, it has made to the way they live since then.

Write up a report on your conversations with them.

Marriage

The marriage ceremony is called the Anand Karaj, which literally translated means the 'Ceremony of Bliss'. Marriage is highly regarded within the Sikh faith. The Gurus themselves were married, apart from Guru Har Krishan who was only a child when he died. They taught the importance of marriage for the stability of the family and of society.

Marriage is seen not only as joining together a man and a woman as husband and wife but as encouraging ties between the families involved. Parents, and other close relatives, will be involved in helping in the choice of marriage partners and they will also contribute financially, and practically, to the expenses of the wedding. After marriage it is customary for the couple to live in the groom's parent's home for as long as they like or until they can afford to set up a home of their own.

Traditionally, marriages have been arranged. The families involved find a prospective partner and suggest to the couple that they should marry. The couple are not forced into marrying someone they do not like or are not happy to marry. The majority of parents love and respect their children and would not want to force them into a relationship with which they were not happy. Family background, education, interests and employment are some of the areas parents consider when suggesting a partner for their child. Photographs are exchanged and the couple usually, though not always, meet. This meeting takes place at the girl's parents' home and involves the prospective couple, their

Reading from the Guru Granth Sahib at a Betrothal ceremony. The Groom is sitting in the front wearing a red turban.

parents and brothers and sisters. Grandparents and aunts and uncles may also be present.

If the couple and the families decide to proceed with the marriage then it is usual to have a formal betrothal (engagement) ceremony. The bride's father, along with a few close relatives will meet the groom's father and relatives to exchange presents for the bride and groom. This meeting takes place in the presence of the Guru Granth Sahib and is a way of making a public declaration of the couple's intention to marry.

After the official engagement ceremony, the mother of the groom visits her future daughter-in-law, in her home, with presents. She places a gold ring on her finger.

The date for the wedding is then set. In India, weddings tend to take place in the open air and so the very hot summer and the rainy season are avoided. In Britain, they take place in the gurdwara and so the weather is not such a consideration. Many take place at the weekend to allow more people to attend.

On the morning of the wedding day, the bridegroom and his family will attend the place decided upon by the bride's family for the ceremony. In India it may be the bride's parent's home but in Britain it will be a gurdwara. A meal is served, but before eating, there is a ceremony to go through. The Milni is a formal meeting of the fathers, grandfathers, and uncles of the couple, which takes place before the other invited guests. The bride's side of the family offer gifts, such as a turban length and sometimes a token gift of money. The Milni reinforces the idea that the marriage unites not only two individuals but two families. A reception meal is then eaten by those present.

After the reception the guests gather together in the presence of the Guru Granth Sahib to witness the marriage ceremony. The groom is asked to come forward and sit facing the Guru Granth Sahib. In Britain he may wear traditional Indian style clothes or a western style suit. Whatever style he has chosen he will wear a special scarf. The bride then comes in and sits at his left hand side, facing the Guru Granth Sahib. A traditional Sikh wedding gown will be red, decorated with gold thread. The granthi then explains to the couple the responsibilities which marriage brings and emphasises the respect which they should show to one another and to other members of both families. Faith in the Gurus' teaching, faithfulness to each other and toleration of one another's shortcomings are necessary for a happy and fulfilled married life. The couple show that they accept that advice offered to them by bowing before the Guru Granth Sahib.

The couple stand, as do the two fathers. A lesson is read and a particular section from page 91 of the Guru Granth Sahib sung:

> *Before taking part in anything, seek the grace of God; By the grace of the Guru, who in the company of the holy congregation expounds truth, success is attained.*

After this the father of the bride places garlands of flowers over the couple. He takes the groom's scarf and ties it to the edge of the bride's duppatta (long headscarf) or places it into her hand. This is the symbol that they are joined together as man and wife. The ragis recite another shabad from the Holy Granth, on behalf of the bride:

> *Praise and dispraise, Nanakji I let pass;*
> *I seize the edge of your garment, all else I let pass,*
> *All relationships I found false.*
> *I cling to you my Lord.*

The couple walking around the Guru Granth Sahib. Notice the special scarf worn by the groom.

A newly married couple receiving wedding gifts.

After this the granthi recites the first verse of the Lavan or Marriage Hymn composed by Guru Ram Das. This composition is four verses long and focuses the worshippers' attention on the spiritual union between God and the individual. It is used as an ideal to be kept in mind throughout married life. When the reading of the first verse is finished the ragis sing it and the couple walk slowly, in a clockwise direction, around the Guru Granth Sahib, the groom leading the bride. They then bow before the Guru Granth Sahib before sitting down to listen to the second verse. This process is repeated through the four verses of the Lavan. After completing the final round, they may be showered with flower petals.

The concluding part of the marriage ceremony involves the singing of another composition of Guru Ram Das, the Anand, the Ardas prayer, a final lesson and the sharing of karah parshad.

The newly-wed couple sit to receive the congratulations of the congregation, who come forward and place gifts of money in their laps to make sure that they have a good financial start to their life together.

A meal is shared in the langar but a reception may also be booked in a hall, hotel or restaurant. In India, the couple often go straight to his parents home after the festivities, where they are to live. In Britain, this also happens but there is now a practice developing of going away on honeymoon before returning home.

Sikh practice requires no formal certificate to say that the couple are married. But in Britain, Sikhs, like everyone else are required to comply with the law which requires the formal and legal registration of a marriage.

Activities

- Interview someone whose marriage was 'arranged'. In the light of what they say, write down what you see as the advantages and disadvantages of arranged marriage.

- Outline the main elements of the marriage ceremony - you could do this in written form or you could draw a series of pictures.

Activities

Key Elements

1 a) What is the marriage ceremony called?
b) What do the Punjabi words mean in English?

2 Which Guru was not married and why not?

3 Describe what happens during the formal betrothal (engagement) ceremony.

4 Describe what happens during the wedding ceremony itself.

Think About It

5 In groups, discuss your understanding of marriage. You should think about the following questions:
a) What do you think makes for a successful and happy marriage?
b) What are some of the pressures which married couples might face?

c) Why do you think that some people choose to get married and others choose not to?

6 How do some of the things which happen during the ceremony point to what Sikhs believe about marriage?

Death

Sikhs believe that death is within the will of God and that consequently it should be seen as an ordinary part of life.

When a death occurs one of those present will close the eyes and mouth and place the arms and hands down either side of the body, covering it with a white sheet. Relations and friends are informed as soon as possible and condolences and support are offered to the immediate family. On the day of the death no cooking is done in the house, relatives and friends bring food in and look after any children.

The funeral service takes place as soon as possible after death but it may be delayed, for example, in order for a close relative who is living abroad to return. Sikhs are usually cremated but where this is not available burial is allowed.

The bereaved family are encouraged to mourn but also to remain calm and peaceful, trusting in God. The Sukhmani, a shabad focusing on peace, often proves to be a comfort during this time.

Before the funeral the body is washed and dressed by people of the same sex. If the person who has died had been initiated into the Khalsa this clothing includes the Panje Kakke (Five Ks). In the Punjab the body is placed on a bier but in Britain it is placed in a coffin. It is then covered with a shroud. In the Punjab it is carried in procession to the cremation pyre, where the fire is lit by a close relative. In Britain, undertakers' cars are often used. The deceased will be taken, sometimes to the gurdwara, but more often directly to the crematorium. A prayer is said for the peace of the dead person's soul. The Kirtan Sohilla (the evening prayer) and the Ardas are read by the granthi or one of the mourners as the body is disposed of in the fire. It is customary for those who have handled the body to take a bath before doing anything else, whilst the other mourners will simply wash their hands and faces.

The Kirtan Sohilla expresses what Sikhs believe about death:
- that every person is a part of God and will eventually return to God;
- that the soul never dies;
- that by a combination of good works and acts of religious devotion the soul will eventually be reunited with God even though it may have to be reborn many times before that union is achieved.

On returning to the home of the deceased the Scriptures will be read. After a few pages the mourners take some karah parshad and prepare to leave the family. Sometimes it is arranged for the reading of the Scriptures to occur in the gurdwara rather than the home. It is also a common practice to extend the reading of the Guru Granth Sahib to a **septah** (seven day) or a **dissehra** (ten day) reading, thus covering the entire official period of mourning.

During this time friends and relatives will continue to call to give their condolences to the family. Close friends and relatives gather together again on the afternoon of the tenth day as the reading of the Scriptures draws to a conclusion. The official period of mourning is then ended with the sharing of karah parshad.

Ashes of the deceased are usually disposed of by immersing them in running water, in a nearby river or stream for example. When a Sikh dies in Britain, sometimes the ashes are returned to the Punjab for disposal. The Sikh faith forbids the erection of monuments in memory of the dead person and prayers for the dead are also forbidden. This is so that no one may be drawn to worship them and so be drawn away from the worship of God.

A Sikh funeral – the body lies in an open coffin at the front of the Gurdwara.

Activities

Key Elements

1 Describe what happens immediately after a Sikh dies.

2 When should a funeral service take place?

3 How is the body prepared for cremation?

4 What is the official period of mourning allowed for within Sikh tradition?

Think About It

5 Why do you think it is important that a Sikh who has been initiated into the Khalsa is prepared for cremation wearing the Panj Kakke?

6 a) Why do you think Sikhs set aside an official period of mourning after a death?
b) What might be the advantages or disadvantages of such a period?

7 Why does the Guru Granth Sahib play such an important part in the funeral service and during the period of mourning?

8 How does the funeral service reflect what Sikhs believe about death?

9 Why are memorials to, and prayers for, the dead forbidden within the Sikh faith tradition?

10 In groups, discuss what different people in your group think or believe about death and about what happens after death. Listen carefully to what people say and especially to any reasons which are given. What do you think about it all?

Assignments

1 Do further research to explore more fully what Sikhs believe about death and about what happens to the soul after death. Write an essay under the title of: 'Death: a Sikh viewpoint.'

2 a) Find out what one other religion teaches about death.

b) Find out about what a non-religious organisation such as the British Humanist Association believes about death.

c) Compare these beliefs with those of the Sikh faith.

Advice to teachers on visiting a gurdwara

Many Sikhs bathe or at least wash before going to the gurdwara. This will not be required of you or your pupils but you will almost certainly be asked to wash your hands on arrival. Shoes will also need to be removed and head covering worn. Often such coverings are available at the gurdwara, but you should ask those visiting with you to bring their own headscarf/large handkerchief/suitable cap if possible. You will obviously need to prepare the students before the visit as to what is required of them and I have found it useful to avoid embarrassment to have a 'practice run' in relation to the head covering particularly. Both sexes should be 'modestly dressed'. In practice this means that I have asked females to wear trousers or long skirts and long sleeved tops, whilst the boys have either come in school uniform or smart but casual 'home' clothes.

In the presence of the guru Granth Sahib, Sikhs act very respectfully. Ask students to make sure they sit either cross-legged or with their feet pointing away from the Holy Granth, as to do otherwise would be regarded as disrespectful. You will be offered something to eat and drink in the langar and probably karah parshad as well. Some gurdwaras provide biscuits and orange juice, others more traditional Indian fayre. Ask your students to at least try a little, out of courtesy to your hosts.

Prepare questions before the visit and check with the host community whether or not photographs will be permitted. If so, designate a couple of photographers from amongst the group rather than have too many flashes going off at once. Copies of good photographs could be ordered later by group members. As part of the follow up to the visit, make sure that a 'thank you' letter is sent, preferably one contributed to by the pupils.

Inform those visiting with you that alcohol, tobacco and non-prescribed drugs are forbidden within a gurdwara.

Developing a Sikh Artefact Collection

The use of artefacts in the classroom as an aid to teaching and learning has much to commend it. Artefacts can provide a stimulus for learning, as they engage with the beliefs and practices of the faith community under consideration in tangible ways. A religious artefact is important, not only for itself, but for what it means to those whose artefact it is. An artefact should never therefore be presented as a 'curiosity' but as an expression of faith, which both affirms and confirms the adherents in their beliefs, worship and way of life.

Artefacts that might be included in a collection include: -

The Panj Kakke (Five 'K's)
    Kanga (comb)
    Kara (steel bangle)
    Kirpan (sword)
    Kacchera (undershorts)
    Kesh (uncut hair) - a photograph

Pagri (turban) (Generally worn by Sikh men, and some Sikh women, to cover their hair. Before they are old enough to tie a turban, Sikh boys generally wear a rumal.)

Figures and pictures of the Gurus, particularly Guru Nanak and Guru Gobind Singh. (Please note that some Sikhs are sensitive about the use of figures of the gurus, in case they distract attention away from the worship of God. It should always be made clear that the gurus are not worshipped, but are respected as teachers.)

Chauri (This is waved over the Guru Granth Sahib as a symbol of its authority. It will have a wooden, or sometimes a metal handle, with yak hair or nylon attached to it.)

Romalla (This cloth is used to cover the Guru Granth Sahib. Romallas are generally donated by members of the congregation.)

(The Chauri and Romalla can be used to explore the importance of the Guru Granth Sahib for Sikhs.)

Khanda and Khanda Symbol (The symbol appears on many Sikh items, as well as on the Nishan Sahib, the flag which flies outside every gurdwara.)

Picture or wall hanging of the Harimandir

For more information about Sikh artefacts, see:
Religious Artefacts in the Classroom, Hodder & Stoughton, 1992

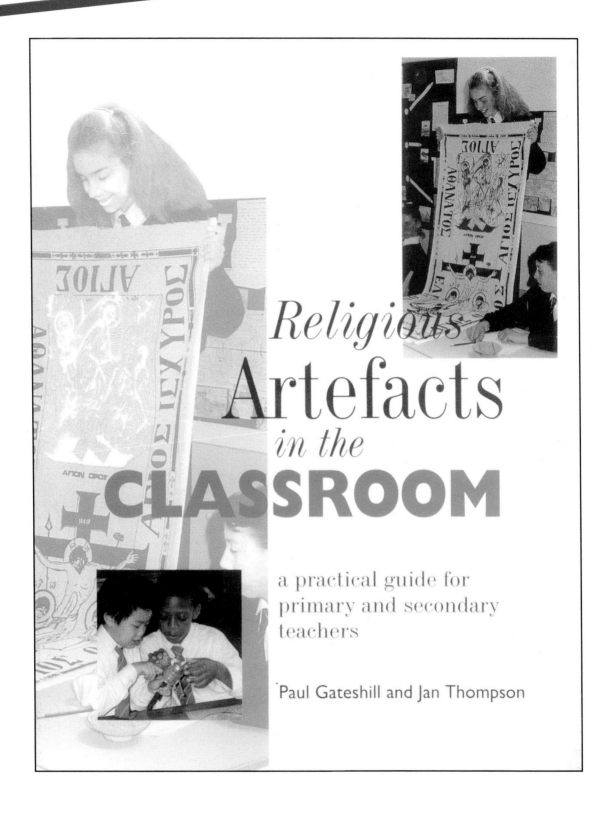

Religious
Artefacts
in the
CLASSROOM

a practical guide for
primary and secondary
teachers

Paul Gateshill and Jan Thompson

Wordlist

Akal Purakh The Eternal One. A term frequently used for God by Guru Nanak.

Akal Takht Throne of the Eternal (Timeless One). The building facing the Harimandir in Amritsar. One of the Five Takhts which act as places of spiritual authority where the most important decisions effecting the whole Sikh community are taken.

Amrit Nectar. A combination of water and sugar crystals used in initiation ceremonies.

Amrit Sanskar The Sikh rite of initiation into the Khalsa.

Anand Karaj (see Anand Sanskar)

Anand Sanskar 'Ceremony of bliss'. Sikh wedding ceremony.

Ardas Prayer.

Baisakhi A major Sikh festival which celebrated the founding of the Khalsa in 1699CE.

Chauri Fan waved over the Scriptures. Made of yak hair or nylon. A symbol of the authority of the Guru Granth Sahib.

Dharam Way of life.

Dasam Granth Collection of compostions, some of which are attributed to Guru Gobind Singh.

Granthi Reader of the Guru Granth Sahib, and who officiates at ceremonies.

Gurbani Divine words revealed by the Gurus. The shabads contained in the Guru Granth Sahib.

Gurdwara The doorway to the Guru. Sikh place of worship.

Gurmukhi From the Guru's mouth. The written form of the Punjabi language in which the Guru Granth Sahib is written.

Gurpurb A Sikh festival which remembers an anniversary (birth or death) of one of the Gurus. Also used of other anniversaries.

Guru Teacher. In the Sikh faith, the title of Guru is reserved for one of the ten human Gurus and the Guru Granth Sahib.

Gutka A collection of around twenty shabads contained in the Guru Granth Sahib. Used by Sikhs in their personal devotions.

Ik Onkar There is only one God. The first phrase of the Mool Mantra. Also used as a symbol to decorate Sikh objects.

Japji Sahib A morning prayer composed by Guru Nanak which forms the first chapter of the Guru Granth Sahib.

Kachera Traditional underwear/shorts. One of the Five Ks.

Kangha Comb worn in the hair. One of the Five Ks.

Kara Steel band worn on the right wrist. One of the Five Ks.

Karah parshad Sanctified food distributed at Sikh ceremonies.

Kaur Princess. The name given to all Sikh females by Guru Gobind Singh.

Kesh Uncut hair. One of the Five Ks. Many Sikh men wear a turban to cover their uncut hair, although the turban is not one of the Five Ks. Some Sikh women also wear a turban.

Khalsa The community of the pure. The Sikh community.

Khanda Double-edged sword used in the initiation ceremony. Also used as the emblem on the Sikh flag.

Kirat karna Earning one's living by honest means.

Kirpan Sword. One of the Five Ks.

Kirtan Devotional singing of the compositions found in the Guru Granth Sahib.

Kirtan Sohilla A prayer said before going to sleep. It is also used of the cremation ceremony and when the Guru Granth Sahib is laid to rest.

Langar Guru's kitchen. The gurdwara dining hall and the food served in it.

Mala A prayer rope made up of 108 knots which many Sikhs use to aid private devotions.

Mela Fair. Used for Sikh festivals which are not gurpurbs.

Manji Sahib A small platform on which the Guru Granth Sahib is placed.

Mool Mantra Basic or essential teaching. the basic statement of belief at the beginning of the Guru Granth Sahib.

Nam Simran Meditation on the divine name, using passages of the Scripture.

Nishan Sahib Sikh flag flown at the gurdwara.

Nit nem The recitation of specified daily prayers.

Palki Canopy over the Holy Granth. Used as a mark of respect.

Panj Kakke The Five Ks. Symbols worn by Sikhs.

Panj Piare The five beloved ones. Those first initiated into the Khalsa by Guru Gobind Singh: those who perform the rite today.

Punjab Land of five rivers. The area of India in which the Sikh faith originated.

Ragi Sikh musician who sings compositions from the Guru Granth Sahib.

Raheguru Wonderful Lord. A Sikh name for God.

Rahit Maryada Sikh code of discipline.

Sangat Congregation or assembly of Sikhs.

Sewa Service directed towards the sangat and the gurdwara but also towards humanity in general.

Shabad   Word. A hymn from the Guru Granth Sahib.

Sikh   Learner or disciple. A person who believes in the ten Gurus, the Guru Granth Sahib and who has no other religion.

Singh   Lion. Name given to all Sikh males by Guru Gobind Singh.

Vand Chhakna   Sharing one's time, talents and earnings with the less fortunate.

Index